OUT OF THIS WORLD

OUT OF THIS WORLD
Suicide Examined

Antonia Murphy

KARNAC

First published in 2017 by
Karnac Books Ltd
118 Finchley Road
London NW3 5HT

British Library Cataloguing in Publication Data

A C.I.P. for this book is available from the British Library

ISBN-13: 978-1-78220-487-9

Typeset by Medlar Publishing Solutions Pvt Ltd, India

Printed in Great Britain

www.karnacbooks.com

It's almost time now
It's almost over
Sooner than later
I'll be dead and gone
Out of this world

And I guess that I'll miss
Some of the good times
But it'll be fine for me
To be moving on
Out of this world

Out of this world
And into another
A kinder world
A world that's better
Out of this world

Out of my mind
And out of my body
Nothing will hurt me
I'll be so happy
Out of this world

And you all will miss me
Then you'll forget me
But that won't upset me
'Cause nothing will get to me
Out of This World

Out of This World
Words and music by Loudon Wainwright
Copyright © 1983 Snowden Music
All rights administered by Downtown DLJ Songs
All rights reserved. Used by permission
Reprinted by permission of Hal Leonard Corporation

CONTENTS

ACKNOWLEDGEMENTS

Many people have helped and supported me in the writing of this book. I'd like firstly to acknowledge the patients I have seen for psychotherapy who have helped me identify a growing concern and interest in suicide over many years of clinical practice and also my colleagues in the East Midlands Psychotherapy Group: Pat Bryant, Sue Neat, Mandy Roland-Smith, Amal Treacher Kabesh, Maggie Senior, and Ann Shotter, all of whom have supported and informed my interest in this area of work for several years.

In particular I would like to thank Professor Andrew Samuels and Professor Mick Cooper for their initial enthusiasm and helpful guidance on publishing and Darian Leader for his support and extremely helpful and detailed comments on the text. My gratitude and thanks also to Dr John Stevens, Elisabeth Rodeck, Jenny Vaughan, Ann Sawyer, and Virginia Everson for reading the MS and for their specific comments.

A thank you also to fellow trustees of CPC (Counsellors and Psychotherapists in Primary Care) Suzy Jackson, Jane Rosoman, Sara Pickford, Jane Monach, and Jane McChrystal, all of whom encouraged me in, and contributed to, the development of the material. My grateful thanks also to the two charitable trusts: the James Wentworth-Stanley Memorial Trust and the Matthew Elvidge Trust, which funded and supported the delivery of the CPC *Working with Suicide* training programme and to Clare Milford Haven for her specific comments. My thanks also to Sissy Lykou for her excellent contribution to the training. Much of the content of the book has been enhanced and developed from the ideas generated in discussion on these CPC training days which were delivered to universities throughout the country. I thank the many delegates who contributed during the training for their intelligent and thoughtful reflections on this complex and difficult subject.

My thanks also go to Clare Bevan for her constancy and perfectly attuned companionship always and, more specifically, while writing in Devon, to my friends Jackie Scruton, Lizzie Haines, and Nina Kaye for the thoughtful interest they showed in the work and to R. for his hidden shallows. And I particularly want to thank my son Lawrence for his wholehearted support, enthusiasm, and unabashed pride in his mother's efforts!

I must also thank the staff of Karnac Books wholeheartedly for getting behind the project and for all their hard work during the production process.

Finally I reserve my greatest thanks and gratitude to my dear friend and colleague Katy Rose who has provided me with so much professional and personal support over the years, who has taken so much of her time to read and discuss my ideas in detail and who has never failed to offer thoughtful and generous help when I have needed it.

ABOUT THE AUTHOR

Antonia Murphy is a psychotherapist and supervisor, with over twenty-five years of clinical experience in the NHS, the third sector, and private practice. As well as her clinical work, Antonia managed the primary care counselling service in Derbyshire from 1998–2006, and was a founding director of Counsellors and Psychotherapists in Primary Care (CPC). Her training portfolio includes course design and delivery of CPC's multi-modality supervision training programme, and more recently she has developed her long-term clinical interest in working with suicide into a training which has been delivered to more than forty universities and other settings. She is the former editor of the *Journal for the Foundation of Psychotherapy and Counselling*, an editorial board member of the *Journal of Psychodynamic Practice*, and co-author (with Joan Foster) of *Psychological Therapies in Primary Care: Setting Up a Managed Service*. Antonia works in private practice in Nottingham.

INTRODUCTION

In danger the holothurian splits itself in two;
It offers one self to be devoured by the world
And its second self escapes.
In the middle of the holothurian's body a chasm opens
And its edges immediately become alien to each other,
On the one edge, death, on the other, life.
Here despair, there hope.

—From Autotomy by Wislawa Szymborska

To my mind this short extract from this startling poem, appropriating as it does the biological term autotomy—the capacity of certain organisms to give up wholeness in order to preserve life when under threat—conveys and captures beautifully that most perplexing and haunting of human impulses, namely the suicidal impetus. I open with this because throughout this book I want to examine suicide in detail but in particular I want to emphasise the horribly paradoxical truth about it-that it is an action *both* for the self and against it. It can be understood as an attempt to save the self but that in turn destroys the self's body (Campbell & Hale, 1991). The suicidal person is making a sacrifice of herself in order to achieve the other side of the bargain—the fantasy that a better future awaits the post-dead self.

There are of course many types of suicide and suicidal acts. There are suicides which come from a long and painful struggle with illness, with misfortune, with disturbance, with despair, with perversion. There are suicides which seem to come from "out of the blue", which are reported by those near to the suicidal person as totally unexpected. There are suicides which are talked about often but never acted on until the final act. There are so-called heroic suicides, altruistic suicides, vengeful suicides, suicides of despair, nihilistic suicides, political suicides, mass suicides, terrorist suicides, suicide pacts, and copy-cat suicides. Just reading this list it is clear that it is hard, and perhaps foolish to try to make generalisations both about what suicide is and about why people take their own lives in such tragic and sometimes horrific ways—suicides vary in the reasoning of the suicidal person, and in their intent. But the one thing all suicides have in common is their destructiveness—the one thing we cannot dispute is that suicide, if it is successful, results in a death.

For many of us it might be easier to think of suicide, if we can face thinking about it at all, in a way which associates it with a depressed or pessimistic state of mind. This reasoning allows us to be sympathetic to suicide and the suicidal, and to relate to its awfulness, its tragedy, rather than to its destructiveness. We can more easily imagine the suicidal person as having given up on life, as having been driven to this dreadful point of no return, perhaps due to unbearable difficulties and challenges. And of course this is in part the case for many suicidal people. In fact most of us can identify with this way of thinking about suicide—who hasn't woken up alone either literally or figuratively, on a bad day in a bad place with a whole of lot of hassle ahead and thought, no matter how fleetingly, of getting out of it all? The mind is saying "I can't stand this." As Cesare Pavese stated (1950): "No one ever lacks a good reason for suicide."

Another way in which we might try to get an acceptable handle on suicide is to adopt the rational position—that the person has considered all options and has "decided" that suicide is the rational choice: a convenient "untruth" which perhaps offers more in the way of making us feel a little less uncomfortable with suicide than a proper or more complete account of the act itself.

What these explanations and rationalisations, though partly true, all miss, and I think are intended to miss, is the violence, the destructiveness, and the sheer scale of disappointment behind the act—a scale for which the word disappointment is not remotely strong enough by any stretch. Edwin Shneidman, the eminent suicidologist who writes lucidly, clearly, and knowingly on suicide, speaks of the suicidal person as having *thwarted* psychological needs. This word "thwart" comes very close to describing the outrage and absoluteness of the suicidal person's sense of life being against them. Their rage about this may not be at all conscious—this is another nasty twist in the suicide tale—but nevertheless, underlying the reasons they may give for their suicidality lies a darker outrage. This leads to the other vital point that Shneidman makes, namely that the suicidal condition is in the main a psychological condition—it is as he says "chiefly a drama of the mind" (1996, p. 4). Thus, following on from this, the key to understanding suicide, to working with it, and in some cases to preventing it, is to explore, elaborate, and bear the particular suicidal person's story in mind, both their real story and their fantasy. In other words to offer the suicidal person the conditions in which it might be possible to find out about this often disturbing drama of the mind, to bring into consciousness their feelings and memories, potentially enabling them to face and to tolerate what has previously been intolerable to and for them.

In this book I take a position in relation to suicide—notwithstanding the many advances in neuroscience, in medicine, in pharmacology, in law, in society, in political engagement we are able or willing to make—that the key to working with the suicidal person is in an understanding of the struggle and frustration in this particular individual's internal psychological world as a result of their coming into and continuing *in* the world *as they see it*. The story of suicide is an individual and a human one—yes, suicidal people have aspects in common with each other—but their own specific drama of the mind is in essence individual at heart.

Being suicidal is not a simple business in any way. There is no obvious or achievable algorithm which will determine whether, when, or how a person is at risk of suicide. Suicide is a complex, perplexing, and deeply unsettling business. Much like life really. Certainly there are groups of people who can be categorised as being more at risk of suicide: those with serious mental illness, those with a history of alcohol and drug addiction, but these are perhaps correlations rather than causes. But concentrating resources on these so-called "high-risk" groups somewhat misses the essential understanding about suicide that is necessary but often avoided within our national health, social, and forensic services—namely that being suicidal is not necessarily an illness and as such it cannot be effectively treated within a formal medical model only. It is important to note that there is currently debate within psychiatry itself concerning the prevalence for yet more diagnostic categories of mental illness, many of which may be misdiagnoses or diagnoses as masquerades for what may well be understandable and necessary, albeit painful, human responses. This is a very serious point and relevant to any exploration about how we respond to the suicidal which I will explore more in later chapters. Suffice to say we cannot understand suicide by simply equating it with mental illness and we cannot help a suicidal person simply by diagnosing them within an exclusively biological framework—much more knowledge and understanding from us all is needed in this difficult terrain.

Perhaps one of the main reasons we reach for medical solutions to the problem of suicide is that it is altogether too frightening and too difficult for us to try to face. We live in an increasingly risk-averse society, certainly here in the UK. With this comes a compulsion to get swift and predictable results and to get rid of undesirable and unwanted human behaviour—to reduce us all to manageable units of wellness or illness, to rationalise us on measurable scales. There is an increasingly unhelpful emphasis on overall well-being and happiness. This gives rise to fantasies that we can and should all be fixed and this in turn champions treatments that only treat surface problems. With suicide this approach can be particularly detrimental. Often an injunction to "get better" and an approach that emphasises the imperatives of positive thinking can be exactly the opposite of that which a suicidal person needs, reinforcing the person's very painful sense of failure and earlier experiences of abject disappointment. The person, the patient, will always know more about themselves and their psychological pain than anyone else even if they don't know how to know this! They may well need a lot of help finding out what the "matter" is. The suicidal act means something, it is about something, something vital paradoxically. It is up to us to help them work this out, not just try to make it go away. In so doing we have a much better chance of transforming the suicidal impulse into something manageable.

So this book is a book about suicide, about knowing more about it, recognising it, acknowledging it, and above all reducing our fear about it and indeed, in some cases, reducing its claim on you. It is aimed at helping you, whoever you are, fear suicide much less so that if you are someone who is suicidal you can get the help you need; if you know someone who is suicidal you can enable him or her to get the help they need; and if you are someone who works with suicidal people you can continue to do this in a more confident, contained, and informed manner. It is also, selfishly, a chance for me to explore and develop many of the ideas I have garnered over the years concerning suicide and suicidal ideation. These ideas are drawn from over twenty-five years of clinical experience working with patients and they stem from a broadly psychoanalytic framework. Many of my patients past and present have at times been suicidal and/or preoccupied with suicidal thoughts, but none of them has as yet acted on these impulses and inclinations. One of the reasons for this may well be the containment that psychotherapy provides as well as other considerations—that the actively suicidal often do not find their way into psychotherapy or leave before the work starts to impact on real psychological change. And of course this work is also drawn from my own personal experience, reflections, and research.

We will never rid ourselves of suicide. We are sentient and so we are able to contemplate it and tragically we are able to act on it. But at the same time we can treat it respectfully, we can take it seriously and not shy away from it. We can be more open and transparent about it and avoid being overly sentimental, simplistic, or condemnatory. It is lonely enough feeling suicidal without the additional isolation of the fear others have of it. We can understand it and we may even be able to reduce it. Suicide prevention is most enabled by more professionals being skilled in working with those who are suicidal and by society being more confident about embracing it as a regular cause of death. Suicide is not particular in terms of race, gender, sexuality, age, wealth, class, religion, or political affiliation, although the imperative that is felt can be amplified and reinforced by any number of external factors. Death by suicide occurs in all walks of life and at all stages of life. Understanding suicide and resourcing those who are able to offer help, support, and treatment to the suicidal is everyone's business. So although I hope those who work with the suicidal will find the book of benefit, it has not been written just for such professionals, but for everyone who has an interest in knowing more about this deadly condition and who may themselves be contemplating or planning suicide or have been affected by a suicidal death.

And what of my credentials for writing this book—why am I drawn to the subject, why am interested in it? I suppose in a way the answer is manifold. On January 26, 1983 my sister Olivia killed herself, aged twenty-seven years. In some current discourses this makes me a survivor of suicide, but this is not a term I would use myself. Olivia's death by suicide had a huge and profound effect on me; she and I were very close in age and in life—I was twenty-six when she died. I have continued to live a full life since her death, albeit on a path that shifted incontrovertibly as a result of her death. Yes, in some ways I am a survivor of her death in so much as her death was an attack on the family. But Olivia's suicide was her story not mine, and *her* very individual psychological history lies behind it. To draw on Shneidman's idea of thwarted psychological needs (1996, p. 18), Olivia had a lifelong sense of feeling and being psychologically and emotionally thwarted.

Which brings me to my second reason for writing this book—I am a psychotherapist. I entered my own psychoanalysis not long after Olivia's death, to help myself bear what remains the most personal catastrophe I have suffered to date; to make sense of what took her to the point of no return; and to examine the history we had shared and to face my own problems which resulted in part from that same shared history, but which took a very different form to hers. I don't think I would have taken this path, and made the discoveries I have subsequently been able to make, and risk the illumination and challenge therein, were it not for her death, for which I thank her, oddly enough. I do wish that I knew then what I now know. I would have known more about the help she could have used, how to get it, and how to respond better to her. But I will never know if this could have saved her.

And my third reason is that I am not frightened by suicide. It concerns me, it disturbs me, it distresses me, but it also intrigues and puzzles me—I want to understand suicide and in so doing do something to help those who get lost in its terrible grip. Certainly I am able to feel fear when working with a suicidal patient—it is an extreme and deadly state—but just the same I want to be able to work with it in the same way I work with any aspects of a patient's mental state.

I have worked with suicidal people over many years both as a psychotherapist and in a voluntary capacity. And unfortunately I think suicide does scare those who work in psychotherapy, counselling, and allied professions in a way that can be unhelpful because it encourages avoidance. But we badly need people to be prepared to face up to suicide and all that lies behind this awful, deadly act without worrying that they are going to be called to account in accusatory and defensive ways. I feel that truly sound work with people who have suicidal acts in mind is badly neglected in my profession as well as within the whole health and social care project. Having said that, happily there have been thousands whose lives have been saved by the help they have got from counsellors, doctors, mental health workers, psychiatrists, psychotherapists, and of course the Samaritans. There are a whole range of professionals and volunteers who are well placed and well informed to help the suicidal amongst us.

In the last two decades I have been a director of a small professional body (Counsellors and Psychotherapists in Primary Care) which amongst other things offered continuing professional development training to experienced counsellors and psychotherapists working mainly for the NHS but also in other settings. These are well-trained and experienced colleagues. From time to time we would ask what topics people would like us to develop as part of this CPD programme. In the early part of the millennium there was a rise in concern, and a subsequent increase in training, in risk assessment within primary care and mental health services. Questionnaires and outcomes measurements sprung up like Topsy and they have ranged from the downright crass to the useful. As a result many colleagues became better skilled at identifying the risk of self-harm, suicide, or harm to others but were often left profoundly unsure as to how, or whether, to offer psychological work once the Pandora's box of suicide or murder had been opened. Do not ever believe those who suggest that counsellors in primary care work with the worried well! Perversely, in some primary care services it was as if once you uncovered some risk of harm this was regarded as a contraindication of taking the person on for therapy. This has now become even more Kafkaesque with the invention of the new improving access to psychological therapies services (IAPT). We now find ourselves with more sophisticated ways of identifying the risk of suicide but a profound sense of unease and disquiet among professionals as to how or whether to work with such patients and an anxious urge to disclose suicidal risk at the expense of the safety and use of the therapeutic frame in case the clinician is charged with being complicit or at worst negligent. I fear this impetus to disclose any hint of risk may become mandatory for some therapists which undermines the specific effectiveness of the privilege of necessary confidentiality within the psychotherapeutic frame.

Furthermore, many experienced and well-trained psychotherapists have told me that suicide per se was not covered on their training courses. So having identified the need for further training CPC developed a training on "Working with Suicide"—an area in which I had always held a deep and personal interest. In advancing this CPC was supported by two charitable trusts—the James Wentworth-Stanley Memorial Trust and the Matthew Elvidge Trust. Suicide leaves a particular and horrible scar on families bereaved by it. Thus the charitable world is peopled by those who have suffered such a loss and who have felt motivated to set up a charity in memory of their dead loved ones. This book then brings together many of the ideas developed throughout the years I have been privileged to offer this training. I am hugely grateful to both these charitable trusts, to my colleagues at CPC, and for all those who have attended the training and contributed so fully and honestly to the ongoing development of these ideas.

So this is a book which I hope will focus your thinking about suicide in all sorts of ways and will enable you to understand much more about suicide, and in so doing to be less fearful and more confident in talking about it with the person concerned when the need may arise in whatever capacity. This may be a lot more frequent and close at hand than you think. Fear is a constriction to useful and purposeful examination. The book expands on the reality behind working with those who are suicidal and tries to offer a deeper psychological exploration of the suicidal mind. It is a book I have been waiting a long time to write and it is one which I hope you will enjoy as well as find illuminating and helpful about a subject which is too often cast into the hinterland because of the understandable fear and unease suicide arouses in all of us.

CHAPTER ONE

Why suicide?

J., a forty-one-year-old nurse, kills herself by taking drugs which she has stolen from her workplace. No one close to J.—her partner, her children, her siblings, her friends, her colleagues—knew she was actively suicidal although she had been low and depressed and anxious at times. Others described her as bubbly and outgoing, always there for others, and expressed shock and astonishment at her death. She had been seen by her GP, but not within the last six months, and had been prescribed antidepressant medication. She recently made an appointment with her GP but did not attend it.

This is not an unusual suicide. Just take a minute to think about your family, friends, colleagues, and neighbours. Do you know any among them, past or present, who has killed themselves or has lost someone close to them to suicide? I expect you do. Pretty much everyone knows someone who is suicidal or has been affected by a suicide, maybe someone very close to you, maybe you yourself. And not all such deaths by suicide are expected, obvious, or readily understandable.

A suicide occurs somewhere every day, in fact every minute. The World Health Organization states that there are over 900,000 deaths every year from suicide—about one a minute. In 2012 suicide accounted for 1.4 per cent of all deaths worldwide, making it the fifteenth leading cause of death. In many countries it is as high as the seventh or eighth cause of death. The WHO also reports that about 5 per cent of the global population attempts suicide at least once. The three-year average rate in the UK for the years 2010–12 was 8.0 suicides per 100,000 but according to the WHO for 2104 it is more like twelve per 100,000. This is lower than average for western European countries. In 2011 this amounted to 6045 deaths by suicide in the UK. According to a survey conducted in 2007 about 17 per cent of people reported thinking of suicide at some point in their lives (McManus, Meltzer, Brugha, Bebbington, & Jenkins, 2007).

Suicide also occurs throughout the lifespan—it is a state of mind that can take hold if you are young, middle–aged, or older. We often think of the young as a high-risk group in relation to suicide—suicide was the second leading cause of death among 15–29 year olds globally in 2012. But this statistic is somewhat misleading since young people do not have high rates of death per se compared with the older population. It is only because overall death rates are so low in young adults (now that diseases such as polio, diphtheria, and tuberculosis have become relatively rare in first world countries) that suicide features as the second commonest cause of death in this age group in the UK.

Suicide can be thought about, potentially, from quite a young age. In other words, as sentient beings, we are able to conceptualise suicide as soon as we can think. And because of this we can, and sadly we do, act on it from quite a young age. Children as young as eleven and twelve have taken their own lives in the UK in recent years, though mercifully this is very uncommon. There were six deaths for those aged 10–14 recorded in the UK in 2012 though suicide is not recorded as a cause of death for children under ten in this country.

So suicide, if not one of the highest causes of death, is certainly up there in numbers which ask to be taken seriously. Over and above this there will be thousands if not millions of other deaths recorded worldwide every year, as accidental or otherwise, which are either direct suicides or indirect suicides. In other words deaths which could not be evidenced as suicide, and therefore were regarded as equivocal, but were in fact suicidal, or deaths that resulted from indirect acts of risk-taking or self-harming behaviours. It seems there is no end to the creativity in which we can be destructive—alcoholism, smoking, drug use, invalidism, sadomasochism, asceticism, antisocial behaviour/violence, body dysmorphia, eating disorders, deadly risk-taking activities, and so on. These are all ways in which an individual can attack his or her life, can shorten its possibilities, can limit the years and race towards death, sometimes horribly and interminably slowly, sometimes horrifyingly quickly. We can think of these deaths as indirect or sub-intentional suicide. But they are impossible to quantify. Add to this the fact that religious or political sensitivities lead some coroners and political authorities to mask suicides, either to protect the family and friends, or to protect the regime or prevailing religious orthodoxy, then we come to realise we are in very murky waters when it comes to declaring any accuracy over the recording of suicide statistics. There is a real difficulty in agreeing criteria for determining a death by suicide and consequently in gathering accurate data on suicide and making international comparisons.

One interesting detail, which appears when suicide rates are examined over time, is that suicide rates go down in periods of large-scale war. In the UK the number of suicides fell during the Second World War and gradually rose again after 1945. War may well provide an outlet for aggression which otherwise is turned against the self (Wertheimer, 1991, p. 4). I will look more at the link between suicide and aggression in Chapter Seven. These days war is a very different matter and modern warfare has brought with it in much greater numbers the suicide terrorist, whose profile is complex and deserving of a particular analysis.

But whatever the pitfalls of garnering accurate data on suicide the numbers tell of a global and constant human phenomenon throughout history. As Al Alvarez describes in his book *The Savage God* (1971), suicide has been with us since we have walked the earth and has taken place over all ages and in all quarters of the earth. There are suicides referred to in the Christian Old and New testaments—Samson's death in the temple could well be described as a suicide, bringing down the building on himself and others. Judas took his life after his betrayal of Jesus and it is arguable that there are suicidal elements to Jesus's own crucifixion and the numerous Christian martyrs thereafter. In the Old Testament (Exodus 20:13) the commandment "Thou shalt not kill" does not point only to murder of another but stands as an injunction not to kill at all—was this written in such a way to encompass the pull of suicide also?

In all societies and cultures from antiquity to modernity, under various religious and political banners, people have taken their own lives for a cause or for allegedly rational reasons. There are numerous accounts of suicide in the ancient worlds of Greece and Rome. John Donne's list of suicides of the classical world runs to three pages and is by no means exhaustive. Alvarez's illuminating book sweeps us across time, race, and cultural diversity, describing as he does suicides among the Iglulik Eskimos to the Marquesas islanders, who believed that a violent death was a passport to paradise. The ancient Scythians regarded it "as the greatest honour to take their own lives when they became too old for their nomadic way of life" (Alvarez, 1971, p. 73). Some suicides in ancient societies seem to have been linked to the notion that bravery and in particular violent death is a "good" and honest act with the act of suicide considered to be either altruistic or heroic or both. Modern society may not embrace the notion of the elderly or ill disposing of themselves so obviously, purportedly to unburden society or families from their care, but if we scrutinise current debates around assisted suicide they are still permeated with this sort of flavour. However, it is important to think about the basis of this belief—who or what is being sacrificed and why the need to make the sacrifice? Many suicidal people appear to believe that the world would be better off without them, and they take the final course of action against themselves with this in mind, or at least in part of the mind. Lying behind this type of self-blaming, self-abnegating suicide is a suicidal fantasy based on a repression of many complex aspects of the person's internal world, one of which is an inversion of rage at what the world has not provided for them. Within the individual this fantasy has, in all likelihood, a long history dating back to early childhood, initiated by the troubled and assailed mind to manage what was psychologically, emotionally, and in many cases physically intolerable. That society can give oxygen to the idea of "not being a burden" is something that we are certainly still wrestling with today. Human history reveals this constant personal and societal inter-play century upon century.

For the ancient Greeks there was an attempt to rationalise suicide and to place considerations about suicide within the study of philosophy and within the law. In Plato's *Phaedo* the philosophical discussion begins as Socrates's remarks that a true philosopher ought to welcome death but that suicide is not legitimate—we should wait until we are called by the gods to our death and be happy to go. He goes on to explain that we are the possessions of the gods, and so have no right to harm ourselves, to go against their intention. However, Socrates himself was later subjected to trial perhaps because of his unorthodox views, found guilty, and sentenced to death by drinking a draught of hemlock. Reports suggest that he took the liquid "like a glass of wine" and may well have accepted himself as a scapegoat or acted out of suicidal desire himself, to accept a legal case for his own death. "… the achievement of the Greeks was to empty suicide of all the primitive horrors and then gradually to discuss the subject more or less rationally, as though it were not invested with much feeling one way or another" (Alvarez, 1971, p. 80). But what these accounts and rationalisations from bygone times indicate is a great sense of distance from the feeling within suicide, from internal conflict and from individual personal pain. Also what they miss is the sense of the ordinary, pitiable misery of the suicide. And even more so they miss the fatal mistake in the individual suicide—that the person will not be around to receive the honour/social benefit/approval/relief of envy etc. that they seek through the act. The apparent rationalisation misses this so fatally.

If we also look at attitudes to death as well as suicide in history we cannot but face the fact that we are a violent lot! Our contemporary concern about violence in society may well be misunderstood as is illustrated by a constant human appetite for violence—gladiatorial entertainment, public executions, beheadings, etc.—on a gruesome scale throughout history and the globe. The Icelandic sagas of the twelfth century are a steady stream of violent dismemberment and tit for tat killings that make modern gangland killings look tame by comparison (*Njal's Saga*, anonymous). But death today has become almost shocking and taboo. It occupies a weirdly abstract but alluring place on our television and cinema screens but in private it is often avoided. Real death, as opposed to televisual death, seems harder to face or accept these days. Darian Leader makes this point in his book *The New Black* (2009), in which he examines modern ideas about depression, making the case that loss, mourning, and melancholia lie at the heart of our contemporary misunderstanding of depression as "illness". Leader links the disappearance of societal/public mourning rites and rituals— the importance of mourning and grieving in public, in a triangulated relational set-up if you like—with the casual proliferation of images of death and violence on our nightly television sets.

> Most Western human beings in fact watch images of death every night in the TV shows about crime scene investigation and murder that fill up the evening programme schedule. It is amazing to realise that this is what most people do after work; they watch programmes

in which someone dies and whose death is subsequently explained and made sense of. The fact that this is reiterated endlessly suggests that death is ultimately *not something that can be made sense of*. And that the increasingly violent images multiply in the absence of a symbolic framework that might mediate them. (2009, p. 74; italics added)

And I would add, if death itself is becoming less available to us to understand and tolerate, where does this leave our capacity to understand and tolerate suicide?

Fictional and literary suicides abound, by which I mean suicides created in literature as opposed to artists themselves who have died by their own hand. From Jocasta, Oedipus's mother, Shakespeare's star-crossed lovers, Madam Bovary, and Anna Karenina, to contemporary scenes of suicide in movies and soap operas. There can be no debate that suicide plays its part, and occupies us creatively, in our intriguingly embattled relationship with life.

Suicide has also been examined in other useful, albeit nonpsychological ways, in particular in Emile Durkheim's exhaustive study *On Suicide: A Study in Sociology* written in 1897. It is almost as if Durkheim heralded the possibility of thinking about suicide in a secular "scientific" way. His perspective was largely sociological—he is often referred to as the father of sociology—and not psychological, written as it was just before Freud, and as such has influenced our thinking about suicide as largely linked to social causes. His work came at a time when scientific thinking was pre-eminent and when, like many thinkers of the day, there was a wish to make scientific sense of things and to move them beyond the hold of religion and/or irrationality. It is a rigorous and masterly piece of research in which he undertook and analysed an enormous amount of data on contemporary suicides across Europe.

His main argument was that suicide is not an individual act but a social fact that was tied to social structures driven by social causes, however hidden they were. He sought to establish that what looks like a highly individual and personal phenomenon is explicable through the social structure and its functions. However, he showed great insight into the state of mind of the suicide. For example, he describes "Melancholy suicide—this is connected with a general state of extreme depression and exaggerated sadness, causing the patient no longer to realize sanely the bonds which connect him with people and things about him. Pleasures no longer attract."

Durkheim's thesis was that every suicide could be classified into three general types—egoistic, altruistic, and anomic. Both the egoistic and the altruistic suicide would, according to Durkheim, be related to the extent to which the individual is integrated into society—too little or too much. The anomic category, however, is connected with an individual's change in relation to society, how she manages or reacts to social change—in other words to loss of wealth, work, or social position, or by contrast significant gain in wealth or status. The overarching intention of Durkheim's work was to move suicide from being seen as an immoral or an unacceptable individual act, as it was by the time he was writing in nineteenth-century Western Europe—things had moved a long way from the rationalism of the Roman Stoics—into a fact about the individual's relation to society. Inevitably this links to a concentration of thinking and of politicising about society and to the idea that suicide could be "cured" by social planning, by social improvement. Of course to some extent this is true and always so. As I write we are in the middle of a period in the UK of abhorrent political and societal abdication when it comes to the care of the elderly, the sick, the poor, the disabled, the refugee, which is causing all sorts of hardship and intolerable suffering to many individuals, *but* this is not the whole story when it comes to a suicide. The suicide creates her own rejection of and from society—she has withdrawn from every offer of help, has closed down, and said no. And this is due to the drama being played out in her mind, not to the lack of help available or to society's indifference or tolerance of suicide, although of course this contributes to her fury and sense of rejection.

But when we roam from the heroes of ancient Greece to the Stoics, the ultimate rationalists, to the Christian and Islamic martyrs, through to Durkheim's sociological explanations, perhaps we miss the individual's internal despair, and we make the understandable mistake of wanting to explain suicide in sociological, political, and philosophical terms. These sociological and historical accounts and theories are fascinating and interesting but they do not attend to the long, slow, deeply hidden psychological process that leads to an individual taking his own life. External events of course play a part, they may explain the "why now", the immediate and present cause, but not the "why", not the long, lonely, mysterious, layered, dark heart of suicide. Camus wrote of suicide in the most individual and creative of terms: "An act like this is prepared within the silence of the heart, as is a great work of art" (1942, p. 3). In an important way external problems have very little to do with suicide—the wealthy commit as much suicide as the poor—in fact broadly speaking statistics on suicide show higher rates in wealthier countries. Wealth does not insure against suicide and suicide is not an escape from external material poverty but rather an escape from internal poverty. Perhaps what these theories and theses offer us is a way to assuage our terrible sadness, anger, or guilt. They offer us something to get hold of when in actual fact the suicide is often most unaccountable to the outsider. What the suicidal person is actually saying they cannot bear seems more or less ordinary, sometimes even banal, albeit impossible for them to bear. The real motives and examination belongs to the internal world which is mostly hidden from others and largely hidden from the person herself as in the opening detail of J.'s suicide. Whether we think of suicide as emanating from despair, bravery, altruism, ultimate rationalism, or from manipulation, all of which assumptions may well be partly true, they all fail as a central understanding of suicide—they fail to recognise the destructive violence of the act and that it is an act both against and for the self.

So if this is the case we'd expect the works of psychoanalytic study and psychotherapeutic writing and literature to be full of theories and examinations of suicide but they are not! Just as a simple exercise I just took every book off my shelves in my consulting room, excluding the specialist books on suicide, and I found extraordinary little reference to suicide let alone any particular theories on it specifically. One explanation may be that the therapist or analyst spends all her time examining with the patient his internal world, his conflicts, his aggression, his hate—so suicidality and the aggression behind it, the ever-present backdrop to suicide, is in the air all the time, either overtly or covertly, in the consulting room, to a greater or lesser extent depending on the patient's internal world. So perhaps even if suicide is not explicitly cited or explored by one or other writer/analyst it is understood and assumed within the wider context of depth psychology, psychopathology, and the extensive theoretical components of the psychoanalytic model—the defences, the unconscious, transference, etc. Those of you who are psychoanalysts, psychotherapists, and counsellors will be familiar with the huge range of theoretical underpinning to this discourse. However, even with this proviso I am surprised that suicide has been so rarely tackled head-on so to speak within psychoanalysis and other related fields.

Having said this of course there is a wealth of theory and under-standing of suicide in the field of psychoanalysis if we think of it in terms of self-destruction and aggression. If we start with Freud—always an excellent place to start—the most notable early reference to suicide came from within the newly established Vienna Psychoanalytic Society in 1910. This was in fact a symposium on suicide with particular reference to suicide among students—which is interesting in itself as concern for suicide among the young still exercises us so much to this day. Clearly the analytic movement at the time was trying to grapple with understanding suicide and in particular our self-destructive drives. Contributors included Freud, naturally, and Alfred Adler and Wilhelm Stekel amongst others. In many ways this marked another turning point in the understanding of suicide, moving it away from Durkheim's social study which related suicide to external societal factors and directing us towards the internal world of the individual, to inner fantasy, and theo-ries about our unconscious.

During this meeting Stekel, a close colleague of Freud at the time, stated his much quoted principle: *No one kills himself who has never wanted to kill another or at least wished the death of another.* Here Stekel is highlighting that which Freud and his associates were so pains-takingly elaborating at the time and thereafter, namely that there are unconscious mechanisms which relate to the repression of impulses, fantasies, wishes, desires, and emotions felt to be unacceptable and which are turned against the self or otherwise, and that the root of these unconscious defences is laid down way back in the very early devel-opment of the child and which are related to the child's experience of how she is received and responded to in the world. In the case of his statement on suicide Stekel is outing the aggressive murderous impulse aimed at an Other (parents/parental figures) or perhaps all Others (the world), which is turned back on the self to become the self-murderous, suicidal impulse.

During this symposium Stekel went on to explore the relationship between the suicidal young person and his parent(s), stating: "The child wants to rob his parents of their greatest and most precious possession, his own life. The child knows that thereby he will inflict the greatest pain. Thus, the punishment the child imposes on himself is simulta-neously punishment he imposes on the instigators of his sufferings."

There is no doubt this analysis gets hold of the aggression but I feel the need to make clear this is not a statement about the truth of any particular parents' role but a truth about the level of repressed rage in the suicidal person and how this is both unconscious and conscious within that person, and a truth about the fantasised parent and child relationship—"the life I should have had". The person does not necessarily understand the source of her own pain or when, why, or how the sense of grievousness took such a hold and became twisted into such a tortured mess out of sight of her own insight. Maybe I feel the need to write that in order to help anyone reading this who has actually lost a child to suicide. For parents whose adult child takes her own life at whatever age this is not something that is theoretically interesting! I do not think there can be any worse a loss. But my need to write that indicates the truth of what Stekel was referring to—it is the worst you can do to yourself *and* your parents and in some cases, but not in all, this is the point of the suicide. This is the suicidal fantasy of revenge enacted.

So here we have Stekel naming aggression at the root of suicide and aggression magnified, misplaced, and misdirected. Freud himself needed to reconcile this elaboration about aggression turned against the self with his earlier ideas about the pleasure principle which had been seen by him as a driving force to the way in which life proceeds. It was later, in *Mourning and Melancholia*, that he elaborated on this puzzle thus:

> So immense is the ego's self love, which we have come to recognise as the primal state from which instinctual life proceeds, and so vast is the amount of narcissistic libido which we see liberated in the fear that emerges at a threat to life, that we cannot conceive how that ego can consent to its own destruction. We have long known, it is true, that no neurotic harbours thoughts of suicide which he has not turned back upon himself from murderous impulses against others, but we have never been able to explain what interplay of forces can carry such a purpose through to execution. The analysis of melancholia now shows that the ego can kill itself only if it can treat itself as an object—if it is able to direct against itself the hostility which relates to an object and which represents the ego's original reaction to objects in the external world. (1917e, p. 252)

He went on to say that "In the two most opposed situations of being most intensely in love and of suicide the ego is *overwhelmed* by the object, though in totally different ways"! I think this is a remarkable observation—in other words the person has lost a vital connection to himself and given up himself to the Other—in the one case, that of love, to the ideal of the Other, in the other case that of suicide to the rejection/ denigration of the Other. Neither of which are true in the external world. No one other person should mean that much to you. But in the grip of overwhelming and extreme emotions that are intolerable to you, that you cannot manage internally, that you cannot regulate on your own, it becomes necessary to act in extreme ways.

Freud's genius was to realise the complexity of the psyche and how essentially destructive as well as life orientated we are. Every aspect of human experience—one's thoughts and memories; one's perceptions of the world and of others within it; all that one says and does; and the ways in which all these dimensions of experience unfold—is shaped and influenced both by conscious, everyday experience and by memories and phantasies residing in the unconscious. We are in fact those who love life as well as hate it, who love ourselves as well as hate ourselves, who love others as well as hate them. And it is this ambivalence, unresolved, unknown, often unrecognised, disallowed, and then enacted which is at the heart of most suicides. It will take many forms and have many complicated roots, sideshows, etc., but essentially this is what we are dealing with when we are dealing with suicide. We may know that each suicidal death is a multidimensional occurrence, predated by all sorts of cultural, biological, biochemical, sociological, circumstantial, relational, real life, conscious elements but in its essence, in the way that it is something we do to ourselves about how we feel, it is in its basic nature psychological.

So can suicide affect every person with equal likelihood? Well, clearly not. Just as with physical pain we all have different thresholds of what we can bear; so too psychological pain—or psychache as Shneidman would call it. "In almost every case suicide is caused by pain, a certain kind of pain, psychological pain, which I call psychache. Furthermore this psychache stems from thwarted or distorted psychological needs" (Shneidman, 1996, p. 4). But much more than just the difference in felt pain, this is also about the context, the soil for our individual development which is fraught with hidden and present elements. Were we a wanted child, a single child, an abandoned child, a sibling, an ill child, a clever child? Were our parents present, emotionally available, old, young, in love or in hate, envious or grateful, kind, fearful? Were they themselves supported or abandoned? I could go on—there is no end to the possible variables of how, where, why and when we come into the world. Intriguingly one child growing up in the apparently same "soil" as her siblings will have a deeply confused and embittered childhood and later life while the others may seem to breeze through life. What are the mechanisms at work here? Whatever they are they are not simple and not able to be replicated. They are unique. And it is in this soil that we need to get down and dirty if we are to respond in any useful way to someone in this kind of pain.

> ... our best route to understanding suicide is not through the study of the structure of the brain, nor the study of social statistics, nor the study of mental diseases, but directly through the study of human emotions described in the words of the suicidal person—the most important inquiry to a potentially suicidal person is not an inquiry about family history or lab tests of blood or spinal fluid, but "Where do you hurt?" And "how can I help you?" (Shneidman, 1996, p. 6)

Of course it is true that with the levels of obdurate, resistant aggression very often present in the suicidal person the answer will be—you can't! But in the context of therapeutic work this resistance itself is the essential psychological twist.

We also know there are so-called high-risk groups—those who may be at greater risk of suicide than the average population—but I often find these categorisations less than helpful because in essence they are circular, as is their treatment. Yes people with alcohol addiction and long-term drug misuse are more likely to die from suicide than others, but why have they become alcoholics and drug addicts in the first place? What was the soil that fermented that lethal pathway? And we know that people with mental health conditions are more likely to kill themselves. But what is the mental health condition, what brought it about in this particular individual? What does it mean to her? What contributes to it being unbearable and unalleviated? These questions are essential in the context of understanding and treating suicide, whatever tangential diagnosis have been made, and I explore the link between suicide and mental health conditions in much more detail in the next chapter.

Also, young people between sixteen and twenty-five have higher than average rates of suicide than other age categories. Useful to know but far more useful to examine what is it about being young that leads to greater lethality and unbearable psychache.

And finally, when asking if we are all equally vulnerable to suicidality, we need to examine the extremely notable difference in rates which exist between men and women when it comes to suicide. Here in the UK, as in the rest of the world, the majority of suicides occur in adult males, accounting for approximately three quarters of all suicides. Latest figures in the UK show the peak difference, both in terms of number of suicides and rate, is in the 20–24 age group, where there are five male suicides for each female suicide. Suicide is the highest cause of death in the UK in men aged 35–45. The organisation CALM, the campaign against living miserably, is a charity which exists to prevent male suicide in the UK. On its website CALM states its aims and values as:

- Offering support to men in the UK, of any age, who are down or in crisis via our helpline and website.
- Challenging a culture that prevents men seeking help when they need it. Pushing for changes in policy and practice so that suicide is better prevented.
- We believe that if men felt able to ask for and find help when they need it then hundreds of male suicides could be prevented. We believe that there is a cultural barrier preventing men from seeking help as they are expected to be in control at all times, and failure to be seen as such equates to weakness and a loss of masculinity.

I would not disagree with this—clearly the statistics demonstrate that men are at much higher risk of killing themselves than women. The current campaigns and strategies aimed at enabling men to come forward for help and to mitigate the cultural/social and gender barriers that prevail in this country are hugely important. Hopefully this work will begin to see benefits not just for men who are suicidal but for men in general in terms of them feeling less shamed about talking about their feelings and less stigmatised if they do. However, we can also explore these differences in gender in relation to rates of suicide in a slightly different way. The data clearly show just how much higher are the numbers of completed suicides for men than for women in all age categories and in almost all countries across the globe (China seems to be the only country showing a significantly different ratio of women to men in low income rural areas, where the numbers are higher for women). But for the most part, if we add together the number of parasuicides—suicide attempts, acts, and incomplete suicides—and actual suicides in the UK, things start to look a bit different. In fact the numbers play out pretty much 50:50 between the genders—women are three times more likely to make an unsuccessful suicide attempt than a man, yet will attempt suicide two to three times more often. So perhaps men are no more actively suicidal than women but they are certainly more successful. In other words there is nothing in the psychological soil of being a man necessarily that is any more likely to lead to *suicidality*, as opposed to suicide, than being a woman. However, there is something in the psychological soil of being a man that is more violent. In 2013, just as an example, out of the 300-plus homicides in the UK, 90 per cent were committed by men. If we look at violent crime overall the picture is similar. And suicide is an act of murderous violence—violence (mis)directed at the body because, as we shall examine in later chapters, no one can really kill the mind without killing the body. To be able to kill yourself properly and completely you need to be able to do violence. If not for any other reason than for evolutionary reasons, men are more prone to using violence to sort out problems, to act on feelings. In this sense we could say violence is gendered—homicide is gendered—suicide is gendered. Men are also more likely to have access to more lethal and effective means of killing themselves due to social, economic, and cultural factors. They are more likely to pick a method that is lethal, and perhaps act out more actively aggressive fantasies than women. Men are also perhaps more conditioned to think that a solution is needed to a problem and soon. Suicide is certainly a solution. They may also feel the pressure of being successful at pretty much anything they do, more so than women, so why should suicide be any different? They will also be susceptible to feelings of shame, of not wishing to have vulnerable feelings, and be more inclined to bury these or deflect them and to keep them well hidden from others for fear of what they will reveal.

In contrast women tend to opt for softer methods of ending their lives—pills, alcohol, cutting, etc., which take longer and may well lead to them being found before death occurs. Men on the other hand choose lethal, instantaneous methods such as shooting, hanging, jumping from a high place or in front of a train. A recent study indicated that a shotgun to the head was the most lethal and one of the quickest ways to die and the cutting of the wrists the least lethal and one of the slowest, allowing as it does plenty of time to be found. We may be able to link the method used in a suicide to the type of suicidal fantasy behind the act and we will explore this further in Chapter Six.

So, yes indeed, the data unequivocally indicates that men are much more likely to kill themselves than women but this does not necessarily mean they are more suicidal in their minds. *Suicidality* is not necessarily gendered but suicide, with its concomitant requirement for efficient violence, is. I make these points not to disagree with campaigners such as CALM but more to emphasise how finessed our thinking needs to be if we are to help individuals, male and female with their suicidality. For example, when assessing men who are thinking of suicide it may well be that we need to ask different questions and ask these questions in different ways than with women. We may also, as CALM and other campaigning groups are doing, establish and promote different ways for men to access the help they need, for example through sports clubs and teams, through contact with other men, through men's social activities and workplace programmes. It is also imperative that those of us in the professions directly in contact with the troubled and suicidal ask directly about plans, methods, lethality, impulsivity, violence, etc. One thing that may be worth noting is that with the growing exposure of women in the public and political domain violence as a response to situations and to difficulties is losing its credibility and acceptability. Alternatives are now much more likely to be discussed and desired. Domestic violence and rape are no longer tolerated in the ways that they once were although there is still much work to be done and in dire times we can often see a regression of such trends. Internationally, torture and capital punishment, while still accepted practice in many regions of the world, are much more likely to be challenged now. Whether this makes a difference to how men feel they have to respond or how they can respond we shall see.

So, to sum up, we take our own lives because we can—we are sentient—we have consciousness and are able to act on what we think we think. And remember suicide is an act both for and against the self. Suicide results largely from psychological pain and confusion and the main source of this pain is imagined, fantasised, and/or real thwarted psychological need which results in huge unrealised aggression and enragement against the world. Suicide is a form of acting out—namely, carrying out an action which is a representation or substitute for something which cannot be expressed or experienced in any other way but which needs to be done to relieve psychological tension or unbearable and overwhelming feelings. This is something we all do some of the time and is particularly prevalent in adolescence when we find ourselves confused and overwhelmed by new, impinging, and conflicting desires and impulses. Looking at suicide this way allows us to imagine why and what it must be like to be brought to this point and also to realise it is quite common to get into this state of mind. The novelist Emma Healey, writing recently about her suicidality as an adolescent, was extremely keen not to apportion blame or even think in terms of who was responsible. In an interview in *The Sunday Times Magazine* (February 1, 2015), she is quoted thus:

> … I don't hold anyone responsible, it was a result of a whole set of unfortunate circumstances, chance if you will, and the reason it's important to underline this is because it happens, can happen, to anyone. I know a lot of people who have struggled with depression or suicidal thoughts during stressful times in their lives—friends and family who have found that preparing for exams or moving to university or starting a new job tips them over the edge. I think it's especially prevalent in young people, because just at the moment when you are discovering yourself, getting used to your new adult body, trying to become independent, and working out fundamental things such as sexuality, you suddenly come under a huge amount of pressure. Choosing subjects at school that will determine your whole future, taking exams, the results of which will allow you to achieve your ambition or close a door for ever, forming relationships that could define your response to others for the rest of your life.

As she says so clearly—suicide happens and there is no one cause.

CHAPTER TWO

Suicide and mental health

Just as I was about to start writing this chapter (February 2015) I heard a very brief piece on the radio relating to the death by suicide of a young woman in an NHS hospital in Manchester. The report emphasised the need for more government spending and resourcing for mental illness. A government spokesperson was then quoted saying (I paraphrase from memory): "This government is committed to increasing spending on mental illness and reducing death by suicide." She then referred to the latest national suicide strategy and followed this with a comment about reducing self-harm. This was of course a well-intentioned response. But it sums up the prevailing problematic orthodoxy that positions suicide as part of mental illness and that elides suicide with self-harm. Look at most current DoH and government documents on suicide and you will see two things: suicide conflated with mental illness and suicide conflated with self-harm. In this chapter I want to critique both these conflations in turn, not because I want to undermine good work but because they are only part of a useful understanding of suicide and because they may seriously divert attention and treatment into potential blind alleys, circles, and missed opportunities when it comes to understanding and preventing suicide.

My worry about the first point—the elision of suicide and mental illness—is that it makes an assumption that at the very outset needs to be challenged. It may surprise many readers to know that more people who take their own lives have never been in touch with any mental health service or even a GP prior to their suicide than those who have. Very approximately one third of those who take their own life in the UK have been in touch with a mental health professional prior to their suicide. But if we accept this as a rough indicator this implies that over half of those who kill themselves in the UK have not sought help, or been referred for help, from mental health services. That is very revealing when we think about how we might best resource and work with suicide prevention. Of course this does not necessarily mean that those who do kill themselves do not have features of what we might call mental illness—they may not have presented themselves to a mental health professional for many reasons. But it should strike a cautionary note over the whole of suicide and mental illness assumptions.

In the UK today the prevailing response to people who are suicidal is based on the belief that an expression of suicidal thoughts or feelings is a symptom or indication of mental illness or is in itself mad. Of course, broadly speaking, emotional, psychological, and mental health difficulties play a huge part in suicide but according to the Samaritans' latest strategy document (2015) only 4 per cent of those who have mental health problems die from suicide. Government and third sector initiatives on suicide prevention almost invariably speak of suicide and mental illness in the same breath. For sure, suicide is strongly linked to despair, to unendurable emotional pain, to complex and chronic social and relational problems, to problems of identity—in fact to all sorts of feelings, conditions, and states of mind. But to call these troublesome states and emotions, even to call suicidality mental illness, is just one way of thinking about them. In many cases it is a useful way no doubt, in as much as it can lead to good help and medication that might reduce the pain. But it can also be misleading. It may also be extremely unhelpful in some cases. All we really know is that people feel and act in certain ways, and often in ways that are not good for them. The rest is down to models and theories. In fact, often very well-intentioned care and treatment models for the suicidal, framed as they mostly are within a mental health agenda, can be felt by the suicidal person to be further exhortations and imperatives to get better in a particular way. This can often increase the impetus for that person to feel she needs to escape and that she failed miserably to fit in with what society/family/work expects of her. This insistence to be what society says you need to be like, to be fixed, repeats something she may always have felt has been missing, an allowance to be as turbulent, vulnerable, hateful, uncertain as she might feel at times—and then how to manage this without inevitable destruction.

Nowadays we often accept an orthodoxy about mental illness per se without enough examination about its assumptions. History shows us there are always outsiders and scapegoats in every society and culture. We are influenced in our rhetoric about mental illness by the desire to have an authority on the subject of our mental health because the whole domain of our mental states, our uncertainties, disturbances, confusions, states of mind, base desires, differences, and in particular these days our relationship to disappointment, arouses fear and rage. Just so suicide. Suicide is a deeply profound and destabilising act which raises strong fears and consequently we have an understandable need for authoritative answers. As Jeremy Holmes, psychiatrist and psychotherapist, says in his poignant lament to suicide after the death of his own close relative: "It is hard to accept that we can be so helpless in the face of unconscious forces over which we appear to have so little control. The challenge to our sense of omnipotence and sense of freedom is overwhelming. There must it seems be an explanation, a narrative, something or someone to blame" (2015, p. 46). We would like answers too for these complex, harrowing, and difficult conditions to lie in other people's hands so that we can disavow ourselves of knowledge and responsibility for these troubles. We can hand it over to the experts. So we either make or become experts. In many ways this is exactly as it should be since none of us can manage everything alone. But then this construction of expertise very quickly leads to a reductive, uncritical, simplistic reliance on scientific and biological determinants to account for and to explain mental functioning. These days it has led to an almost totalitarian dismissal of any approach or treatment within government health services that is not "evidence based". The trouble is, that which is deemed to be evidence based is defined in quite alarmingly narrow parameters. Nowhere is this reductionism more damaging than in the care and treatment of the suicidal.

In 2003 Richard Leyard, a health economist, was appointed by the government to investigate the economics of mental health treatment. His results were understandably shocking—he quotes a lot of numbers—for example, depression is 50 per cent more disabling than angina, arthritis, or diabetes; 90 per cent of those who are suicidal get minimum treatment but 100 per cent of those with heart disease get some medical attention, and so on. The figures from the surveys he conducted and his reports make an urgent and compelling case for much improved spending on treatment for mental health. They are largely responsible for the new Improving Access to Psychological Therapies initiative rolled out in the NHS in 2009. It was clever of the DoH to appeal to a compassionate and thoughtful economist such as Leyard since the numbers were used to convince the Treasury to invest in IAPT. By getting people "better", so the reasoning goes, the government can get back 4 per cent of the GNP lost by the effects of mental illness through lost working days, lost taxes, sickness benefits, parallel physical illness, family functioning, etc.

So that's all good then—or is it? If we examine this further we find some questionable assumptions. In order to quantify and demonstrate that mental illness has a major effect on physical health, Leyard and his collaborator David Clarke undertook surveys to explore people's relationship to *happiness*. So without even needing to read the research we see that these experts are clearly conflating unhappiness with mental illness. In a lecture delivered at the London School of Economics in 2003, entitled *Happiness: Has Social Science a Clue?*, Leyard defined happiness and unhappiness thus: "By happiness I mean feeling good—enjoying life and feeling it is wonderful. And by unhappiness I mean feeling bad and wishing things were different."

I am not sure but does this imply that Richard Leyard believes that "feeling bad and wishing things were different" is a description of being mentally ill? If this is so we are all damned to suffer mental illness forever and a day. And of course in a way it is true—we *are all ill*—we are all ill from a common imperfection, a common flawed humanity, a complexity of emotions and unknowns. The danger occurs when we conflate this broad view of being flawed and troubled or just ordinarily unhappy with something that is called mental illness and all that goes with that in this day and age—psychiatric diagnoses, doctors, medication, etc., in other words the medicalisation of human difficulties and despair. Instead of asking those who are depressed or suicidal such ordinary questions such as "How are you hurting?", "What do you feel is the matter?", "What would you like to talk about?", "What would help you right now?", we instead declare something is wrong with them; we refer them on to a medical professional; we make a diagnosis; we then try to link the problem to something which will fix them. The latter kind of approach assumes that there are conditions to be fixed rather than people who are struggling or communicating about themselves in all sorts of ways, some of which are very disturbed and disturbing for sure. These are quite different and important paradigms. Mostly when it comes to a proper and full examination of the human experience there are no definitive statements to be made about happiness or unhappiness, no absolute answers about how we should feel, no goals other than death—which is hardly a goal but rather an inevitability, no clear sets of instructions. In other words no clear diagnoses of the human condition.

To return to Leyard's definition, it is true that critical thinking and taking responsibility for your life may not make you perfectly happy but you may want to question (critically) whether such an idea of happiness is quite the dream ticket, and whether you want to be considered mentally ill if you don't conform to the government's required version of happiness. As a definition of mental illness and as a way of justifying diagnosis and consequent treatment, Leyard's position is not just simplistic but ludicrous. As the writer Jenny Diski opines in a critique in *The Guardian* newspaper of Leyard and Clark's book *Thrive*, "[T]he desire for everyone to be happy might seem kindly but it can lead to various destinations, including Huxley's Brave New World and cloud cuckoo land!" (June 25th 2014).

Currently there are many claims about mental illness, about what constitutes an illness; there are myriad diagnoses for all sorts of disorders and illnesses; there are long descriptions of the forms these illnesses take linked to biological determinants; there are statements about what causes them, what are the best and most evidence-based treatments, etc. But formal psychiatric diagnostic systems do not necessarily make sense scientifically and, more important, do not necessarily advance our understanding or treatment of mental disorder. As child psychiatrist Professor Sami Timimi argues:

> Unlike the rest of medicine, psychiatric diagnoses have failed to connect their diagnoses with any causes. There are no physical tests that can provide evidence for a diagnosis. Diagnoses in psychiatry are descriptions of sets of behaviours that often go together. By itself a psychiatric diagnosis cannot tell you about the cause, meaning or best treatment. (2014, p. 208)

Let us look at depression for example because of its very close link to suicide. Depression is defined in the Diagnostic and Statistical Manual of Mental Disorders (DSM) thus:

DSM-IV Criteria for Major Depressive Disorder (MDD)

- Depressed mood or a loss of interest or pleasure in daily activities for more than two weeks
- Mood represents a change from the person's baseline
- Impaired function: social, occupational, educational
- Specific symptoms, at least 5 of these 9, present nearly every day:
  1. Depressed mood or irritable most of the day, nearly every day, as indicated by either subjective report (e.g., feels sad or empty) or observation made by others (e.g., appears tearful)
  2. Decreased interest or pleasure in most activities, most of each day
  3. Significant weight change (5%) or change in appetite
  4. Change in sleep: Insomnia or hypersomnia
  5. Change in activity: Psychomotor agitation or retardation
  6. Fatigue or loss of energy
  7. Guilt/worthlessness: Feelings of worthlessness or excessive or inappropriate guilt
  8. Concentration: diminished ability to think or concentrate, or more indecisiveness
  9. Suicidality: Thoughts of death or suicide, or has suicide plan.

DSM-V update has also proposed anxiety symptoms that may indicate depression: irrational worry, preoccupation with unpleasant worries, trouble relaxing, feeling tense, fear that something awful might happen.

So what do we make of this? At best we could say it is somewhat tautologous—depressed mood means you "have" depression! But, more important, the DSM definition of depression is, as Timimi indicates, a description of a set of symptoms and behaviours that are clustered together. It includes feelings and emotions—guilt/worthlessness. And finally it includes a reference to suicidality. But a diagnosis? Of an illness? Really? None of the above are measurable physical differences on any objective scale. There are, however, psychiatrists who take a very different view and who insist that depression is an illness in such a definable way as other physical illnesses. Dr Tim Cantopher says that if he were to draw fluid from the spinal cord of depressed patients he would find a deficiency of two chemicals: serotonin and noradrenaline, neurotransmitters that regulate functions in the body and brain. "Depressive illness is not a psychological or an emotional state and is not a mental illness. It is a physical illness," he writes. "This is a fact not a metaphor" (2006, p. 3). So here Cantopher is going way over to the other side from Timimi and the critical psychiatry lobby—he is putting depression right there with physical illnesses such as diabetes, etc. Which begs another interesting question—if this is so, that depression and bipolar disorder are a result of faulty chemistry, why have a category at all which is called "mental illness"—why divide these illnesses from other so-called physical illnesses? Maybe this is because it is not so simple as Cantopher would have it and that our response to our own mental world, and that of others, is complex and unnerving—often quite literally! It may well be true that the spinal fluid will show differences when we are in a state known as depression but that does not mean it is an illness or that it is best treated as one.

In fact what these claims around a diagnostic illness model for depression fail to consider is that depression itself is a protective defence mechanism which if removed may expose the person to likely and greater intolerable distress. Darian Leader quotes some recent studies which claim "… that mild depressions may actually protect *against* suicide. In other cases, the way that a drug dumbs down a person's mental state may short-circuit the production of genuine defences against suicidal feelings" (2009, p. 15). This could explain reports that some antidepressants *increase* the risk of suicide. We could think of depression then, as a good defence gone wrong—the suppression of psychological pain and conflict that is unbearable so the mind shuts down: a bit like putting yourself in jail to be safe but then not being able to get out when you want—maybe even becoming a bit used to life on the inside where you don't have to face the responsibilities or tensions that arose on the outside. To get out you have to be able to find the key again, be sure it is safe enough to come out, and that the world will tolerate you and help you and that you will once again be able to endure what life throws at you. Once we are depressed we cannot be at all sure of this.

It would appear, not surprisingly, that today's psychiatrists vary widely in their opinions as to the nature of mental illness and its very existence. I think we should be heartened by the continuing debate about this within the psychiatric community. The latest update of the DSM-V brought a veritable hail storm of critical response. The DSM is a manual developed by the American Psychiatric Association but is almost universally adhered to in the UK and elsewhere in the world. Here in the UK the BPS (British Psychological Society) had this to say in response to the latest update: "The Society recognises that a range of views exist amongst psychologists, and other mental health professionals, regarding the validity and usefulness of diagnostic frameworks in general and the Diagnostic and Statistical Manual of the American Psychiatric Association, in particular. However, there is a widespread consensus amongst our members that some of the changes proposed for the new framework could lead to potentially stigmatizing medical labels being inappropriately applied to normal experiences and also to the unnecessary use of potentially harmful interventions" (BPS statement, 2014).

The biggest beef people in the professions have with this latest update, and to some extent with previous versions, is something that has always been troubling about psychiatric diagnosis, to which the BPS allude, namely that the DSM labels as illness much of which is normal at any time in anyone's life.

For example, we can imagine how terrible it is to have, or worse still, to be, a teenager who does not seem willing or able to do anything; who opposes everything; who becomes increasingly antisocial, promiscuous, delinquent, drug dependent, etc. I can only imagine how difficult that is for long-suffering parents, social workers, and the child alike. But to classify this as an illness as given in the new DSM-V as "Oppositional Defiance Disorder" or "Parental Refusal Syndrome"!, and to recommend treatments with drugs based on such diagnoses, is surely to be wandering so far from the point of helpfulness, understanding, insight, love, and support as to completely lose sight of the demonstration the child is making and why. Donald Winnicott way back in 1956 was writing much more radically about this in his paper entitled "The Antisocial Tendency":

> There are always two trends in the antisocial tendency. One trend is represented typically by stealing, and the other is by destructiveness. By one trend the child is looking for something, somewhere, and failing to find it seeks it elsewhere, when hopeful. By the *other* the child is seeking that amount of environmental stability which will stand the strain resulting from impulsive behaviour. (1956, p. 310)

Here Winnicott is emphasising the *point* of the delinquent behaviour, namely that it is a sign of hope—the adolescent is still looking for and trying to get what she needs from the world, and that it is also a request for the world to contain her. I wonder if suicide, particularly adolescent suicide, is in some ways a similar but a tragically final act—an attempt to get the world to know what the young person needs, but also to attack it for not being able to give it.

In fact inventing new mental illness diagnoses not only does not help in terms of improvement but also increases, rather than lowers, stigma. We have the dubious outcome that the patient feels he is stuck with the label and the rest of us think he should/can be treated and cured by the experts. As one patient put it to me: "A mental illness diagnosis sticks like shit." And further to this, and perhaps more controversially, I would suggest that for many of those who accept and even ask for a label this is just what is desired—a way of continuing to seek entitlement, a way of continuing dependency, a way of gaining love, a way of avoiding the terrors of abandonment. In fact it is often *repetition*—to use Freud's term—the painful experience or memory is relived again and again until a sufficient defence has been built up after the event—or not, sadly, in many cases. As he states: "There are people in whose lives the same reactions are perpetually being repeated uncorrected, to their own detriment, or others who seem to be pursued by a relentless fate, though closer investigation teaches us that they are unwittingly bringing this fate on themselves. In such cases we attribute a 'daemonic' character to the compulsion to repeat" (1933a). "The impression they give is of being pursued by a malignant fate or possessed by some 'daemonic' power; the compulsion to repeat can be daemonic. It can turn against the subject to the point of self-extinction" (1920g, p. 21).

So these confusions around what is or is not illness, mental or otherwise, are significant issues for those of us who are suicidal or who have someone in our lives who is suffering in this way, since they have a great deal of bearing on how we are treated and responded to and on what happens next. Some psychiatrists go further still, stating that even illnesses such as schizophrenia, these days more or less accepted by most as a mental illness with organic/biological/genetic determinants, are not even illnesses but social constructions. Mary Boyle, emeritus professor of clinical psychology, writes in her book, *Schizophrenia: A Scientific Illusion*, that schizophrenia is socially constructed; it therefore not only has no scientific status, it is just not the sort of thing than can earn such status. Boyle suggests that what we have come to know as schizophrenia is a result of power imbalances in society. This argument is supported by examples of delusional beliefs that on closer examination reflect prevailing social structures; hallucinations that give voice to perpetrators of trauma. The proper way to assist those currently diagnosed is to help them understand the forces that shape their experience and, presumably by virtue of this, to overcome them. In this Boyle aims to show how even schizophrenia is a deeply problematic concept as illness. As Boyle reflects: "It is unlikely that alternatives to 'schizophrenia' (as distinct from its replacement with equally problematic concepts) will develop and persist unless we face not only the deficiencies of the concept but also the social and intellectual habits which have allowed it to flourish" (1988, p. 317).

Here it seems to me Boyle and others are not making a case for no illness = no problems, but something much more complicated: that alternatives to the illness model may be more helpful for us to embrace but may be very different, and in all likelihood harder for us to manage but potentially more honest. When it comes to suicide I think that is the key and the plea. Adam Phillips, the psychoanalyst and literary critic, writes some very interesting things about madness in his book, *Missing Out: In Praise of the Unlived Life*. In exploring the idea that "our unlived lives—the lives we live in fantasy, the wished-for lives—are often more important to us than our so-called lived lives, and that we can't (in both senses) imagine ourselves without them" (2012, p. xvi), Phillips goes on to examine why and what we call madness: "We call people mad when they are unintelligible and/or when they behave in ways that are excessively disturbing. The mad people are people we can't understand and who do things that are too unacceptable; and so they are people we may be, or feel ourselves to be, endangered by. ... Madness, as the British psychoanalyst John Rickman once remarked, is when you can't find anyone who can *stand* you" (2012, p. 187).

Darian Leader also explores this territory in his book *What Is Madness* (2011), namely that delusory thinking, "irrational" belief systems and "mad" behaviours are not treatable symptoms of a psychotic illness but signs of the individual trying to make something tolerable with his madness; they are ways in which he may be trying to find someone, something that can stand him (see also Winnicott above). These "displays" and ways of being are the mechanisms for surviving, in relation particularly to regulation of desire for "Other", regulating the difficulty around distance and closeness of "the Oher". "Being mad", Leader argues, can be manifest in living quietly and ordinarily for years and years; "acting mad" can be the process of recovery and healing. Modern psychiatry fails to spot this, sees only the florid or overt as in need of treatment; has often stopped really listening to and understanding its patients. And today's politicians and the public of course encourage the idea of fixing the mad. Fixing them quickly and neatly then becomes a requirement of medicine. However, in reality a patient referred into today's mental health service is likely to be treated by several different individuals and services and moved on from one to the other, experiencing multiple assessments and often a variety of diagnoses. Jeremy Holmes makes a plea against this fragmentation and for a return to long-term and continuous care: "There is rarely one single individual who holds the patient in mind through all the phases of their illness, in sickness and in health. No risk assessment protocol can substitute for this intimate knowledge built up over time of patients' unique vagaries, strengths, weaknesses, vulnerabilities and inner workings" (2015, p. 53).

Leader, Phillips, Holmes, and Rickman are all in different ways emphasising both the importance of madness and what it might be for, as well as our fear of being too much, being something that we think cannot be "stood". This has of course an immediate link to being "understood". And to being someone who needs to find an Other who can stand him, as Holmes puts it: "to hold them in mind" through it all and out the other side or not. If we follow on from this to thinking again about suicide we can see the suicidal person as both an example of someone who can no longer stand his "self", someone who feels he cannot be tolerated by others but also someone who is expressing a need to be "stood", someone who is communicating that that is what he is looking for in the "Other". However, the final sting may be that this in itself is a wish or frustration which has to be tolerated and survived rather than one that can ever be fulfilled. Freud tells about the need for us to grow out of a need for understanding and being understood. This may well be life's real challenge and may well be the one that the suicide struggles with, sometimes sadly to the end.

Really whether madness is illness or illness is madness there is no one way to look at these things. As Oscar Wilde said: "Truth is rarely pure and never simple"! To quote Phillips again: "… a repertoire might be more useful than a conviction, especially if one wants to keep in mind that there are many kinds of good life." (1993, p. xvi) There are also many kinds of bad life and many kinds of help we can offer each other when we feel we are in the midst of a very bad time. Psychiatric diagnoses are but one form of this. But we need to be careful that they do not take over from the need to think about these things in a broader, more containing context. For just as there are many who will think of depression and anxiety as illnesses there are others who do not. Having a theory about things, about mind, about self-harm, about suicide, is a way of being able to think about these things. And it is particularly valuable, and particularly difficult, to be able to think when dealing with suicide. This mirrors the reason for the symptoms itself. The person has the symptoms in order to say something about feelings, about their unendurability, and therefore something about the need for relationship and for help. In this way we are mind and body at the same time and constantly negotiating the psyche–soma balance, the inside and outside balance. We are also constantly negotiating our fantasies about self and other, about being known and understood, etc. However, I would suggest that when we are about to kill ourselves we have stopped thinking. We have all but closed down. And by this stage we have been very adept at shutting everyone else off from us too.

The more important truth than whether depression is an illness or not or whether schizophrenia is a social construct or genetically carried is that we are all vulnerable to mental and emotional disturbance at any time given our history, certain events, and circumstances. And we don't know what the circumstances are that will cause us to tip, and if we do tip, when and how far we will fall, how much we will prevent ourselves from being helped, or how much we will accelerate the process. It may well be that some of us are more vulnerable to states of desperation and depression than others, but this is likely to be because of things that have happened to us and things that have not happened for us in our lives rather than a gene or faulty wiring that can be corrected. More important, to take notice of something we call illness is vital. Winnicott talked of our need to be able to tolerate and allow some disintegration. He stated "Flight into sanity is not health. Health is tolerant of ill health, in fact health gains much from being in touch with ill health with all its aspects" (1986, p. 32). In other words health is not an absence of illness or frailty or flaws. It is being in touch with all these aspects. I wonder if we are building a rod for our own backs if we insist too much on being healthy and happy as if being ill and unhappy was somehow a failing or failure and in need of correction. Suicide may increase if we insist on Leyard's version of mental illness, as society becomes more demanding of us in terms of "being healthy" and "being happy", leading us to more exacting solutions. Suicide is, after all, as well as many other things, a solution. The more we experience society's importuning us to be happy and successful the more we may feel a failure and a fury at not being so and find ways of making our escape!

If suicide were an illness, progressive and treatable in the way that other organic illnesses are, we would be much better at identifying this and where people are on the way along the path of suicide. But we are not able to do this. We should not denigrate suicide to symptom status only. Of the large numbers of people who have a diagnosis of depression very few are suicidal. The link between suicide and illness is low. The psychology of suicide is not equivalent to the psychology of depression. Also there is no suicide algorithm, no tool for "showing" suicide although more recent research has led to the development of some helpful and sophisticated risk assessment tools and approaches to the treatment of suicide. We will look at some of these in later chapters. However, it remains that completed suicides are often impulsive but sometimes long term, related to a myriad of complicated, puzzling, confounding, confusing, unpredictable factors—knowns and unknowns. Not more common in those with identifiable mental illnesses than those without and it is often, tragically, a shock to those closest to the suicidal person. It is much better therefore to approach suicide as a standalone condition and in this way gain a clearer understating of it and a clearer approach to its assessment and its treatment.

CHAPTER THREE

Suicide and self-harm

S elf-harm and suicide are often conflated together particularly when undertaking risk assessments within mental health and psycho-logical work but also within health policy initiatives. However, I was pleased to see this comment in the latest government suicide pre-vention document (*Preventing Suicide in England: A cross government out-comes strategy to save lives*): "We also have to be clear about the scope of the strategy. It is specifically about the prevention of suicide rather than the related problem of non-fatal self-harm. Although people with a his-tory of self-harm are identified as a high-risk group (*of suicide*) we have not tried to cover the causes and care of all self-harm" (DoH, 2012, p. 4). What is important in this statement is a recognition of the difference between self-harming behaviour and suicidality. They are not mutually inclusive and for the most part self-harming and suicide do not have the same quality or intentionality although they may have aspects of self-aggression in common.

Self-harm is a term which describes the many different ways in which self-inflicted physical attacks are carried out on a person's body. Implicit in this is the idea that the body is the vessel on which deliberate and usually repeated acts of harm—cutting, burning, marking, bruis-ing, hitting, digesting, etc. are conducted, but that the body is not to be killed. In fact in self-harming, in essence, an act of living is being carried out. These are acts of harming the body and continuing to live are not suicidal acts per se.

In his unapologetically outspoken memoir of his early childhood sexual abuse and subsequent emotional and psychological devastation, the pianist James Rhodes speaks of his own self-harming thus:

> It is a regular consistent, effective coping mechanism. And it is as rife as the not-so-hidden Valium craze of the 1970s. The majority of those who engage in this behaviour are catastrophically misunderstood, misdiagnosed, mistreated. SH is *not* an indicator of suicidal ideation. It is *not* indicative of a threat to others. It does *not* mean that you are less capable of functioning well. (2014, p. 109)

Self-harming is about harming oneself physically in order to cope emotionally, in order to help the self to manage the enormous difficulties of living as oneself when emotions are felt to be too overwhelming or seem unacceptable. As a gesture or action the symptom of harming oneself is very paradoxical. People who regularly self-harm often report feeling relief or more alive from the infliction of pain and injury to their body. This often stems from a certain deathliness or cut-off dissociative state that they feel in their other other wise everyday lives. Such a person may not be able to connect to normal or abnormal feelings or sensations and might have dissociated from some terribly difficult feelings or memories. So the action of cutting or inflicting pain is used to regain a sense of at least feeling something, even if it is pain, and a sense of control over overwhelming feelings or feelings that might otherwise feel out of control. The conditions for such behaviour, which is often highly repetitive, are rooted in our early experience of how our bodies are handled or not handled or abused (by parents and other carers) both physically and psychologically.

In her book *Self–Harm: A Psychotherapeutic Approach* Fiona Gardner makes a compelling argument for the self-harmer as being "encaptive, captivated, drawn into and bound by conflicting desires." The person is in thrall to his repeated behaviour because of an internal bind. She explains that

> Psychotherapy with patients who were cutting revealed this intra-psychic struggle, characterised both by a quality of enslavement

and a longing to cut the ties that so tightly bound this relationship. The patients appeared stuck and imprisoned in an enclave, where they were dominated by conflicting desires. It was as if the cutting represented both the marks of the bondage and the signs of the desire to cut loose and break free.... they appeared to be almost enthralled by this stuck state of mind. (2001, p. 12)

Gardner's ideas reveal that something is going on between the self and the idea of the Other which is characterised by both intense involvement and the wish to get away from this intensity. A bind indeed. And what do we do with the ties that bind? We cut them if we can or we remain trapped by them.

I am reminded here of a patient who had self-harmed habitually, daily, repeatedly, sometimes up to twenty times a day for many years, by bingeing, purging, cutting, and burning, often on the same parts of her body. During the course of her therapy it emerged that she was bound to an idea/ideal of herself as the baby who should save her mother from the impossible grief of her dead sister. Her older sister had died at eight months, about a year before my patient was born. It seems she had internalised an idea, a feeling, that she had to be so important and special in order to relieve the parents of the awfulness of the dead child but also to be something extra special so as not to die on them. At the same time she was also unconsciously trapped in this idea, and hated it for what it made her feel—that she was unworthy of it and deeply abandoned as an ordinary baby. She had always felt she had to live up to this, live with this, impossible unconscious demand. The demand had not been made by her parents in any real sense; they did not say this to her in any explicit way, but it had been felt by them—this baby will be strong and special and will live—and this was taken in by her, into her psyche, from birth.

In this way, as Gardner puts it, the behaviour of those who self-harm demonstrates that "what they experienced was felt as an apparently irreconcilable psychic conflict ... a specific type of internalised relationship characterised both by intense involvement/possession and the wish to get away" (2001, p. 12). Adolescence of course is a time when separation is particularly compelling and rejection is particularly feared, and it is often difficult to journey through it unscathed. It is no coincidence that self-harming behaviours are very common amongst adolescents when often fears of abandonment are re-aroused which are in conflict with, and in contrast to, competing drives towards sexuality, individuation, and separation. At this time there can also be actual feelings of isolation, of not being known or thought about properly, or fantasies that one is all alone and totally misunderstood. Adolescence is also a time when body image is hugely important. Attacks on the body can be a way of managing competing feelings about the body and sexual and other feelings aroused in the body. Freud famously declared: "The ego is first and foremost a bodily ego; it is not merely a surface entity, but is itself the projection of a surface" (1923b, p. 26). Here he is emphasising that the development of the self comes initially from sensations received by the body, especially those received by the surface of the body—the skin. The tiny baby feels almost all his contact through the skin and is contacted and responded to in turn through the nursing mother's touch and feel. "Thus the sense of a skin which can consistently and dependably contain the child's body, with all its uncontrollable sensations and instinctual processes, is established through the combination of various elements in the maternal environment" (Gardner, 2001, p. 67). In turn the emotions in all their various elements are also able to be contained, or not, by the body and by the skin around the body. The self-harmer attacks the very skin which is not felt to be contained or containing enough. Actual bodily changes and impulses experienced during adolescence can be experienced as unmanageable, particularly so if body image has not developed well enough. This links with the suicidal fantasy of body elimination described later in Chapter Seven. At adolescence there is often also an arousal of aggressive feelings which can be very frightening and unacceptable. Self-harming relieves these feelings, cuts the bind, and acts out the aggression on the body.

Suicide too is an act of aggression and violence, unknown, unconscious, often un-named, and turned towards the self. The action is to kill the body in order to act out the death of the life that is not wanted and to act it out in relation to the world that is being rejected. A lot of the time suicide and self-harm have things in common for the person concerned. In an everyday sense continued and escalated severe self-harming can and does lead to the danger of death and actual death. But the self-harmer is *not* saying "I want to die." The self-harmer is saying, "I want to live but repeated self-harm is the only way I can find to bear the pain of living with what I experience inside me and to control what I find impossible to bear about myself and what I cannot imagine anyone else can bear about me." A self-harmer reported: "Cutting is not the problem for me—it's the solution. If I don't cut myself, I can't cope, I feel like I'm going to go crazy" (Turp, 2003, p. 35).

"Relief of feelings" was reported as the most common reason given for self-harming behaviour in the Bristol Crisis Service for Women: *Women and Self Injury Report* (1995). As Maggie Turp points out in her book *Hidden Self–Harm*, we all self-harm to some extent. We all manage the vicissitudes of life variously and with a variable dose of what she calls *CASHAs—Culturally Acceptable Self-Harming Acts*. Sometimes these so-called CASHAs can be suicidal acts too. Back in the 1970s the American satirical writer Kurt Vonnegut declared that "The public health authorities never mention the main reason many Americans have for smoking heavily which is that smoking is a fairly sure, fairly honorable form of suicide." Self-destructive and self-harming behaviours are never too far away from any of us. A feature of self-harm is its close association with behaviour which can be seen as socially acceptable and normal. Think about the relationship between social drinking to alcoholism; recreational drug use to drug addiction; biting your nails to cutting, slashing, burning the skin; skipping breakfast and lunch to anorexia; carelessness to self-neglect; working late to never being able to stop work; playing hard contact sports such as rugby to headbanging, and so on. In thinking about self-harm in this way Turp and colleagues introduce us to a continuum of self-harm and to the notion of self-harm and its links both to self-soothing and to ritual. Self-soothing and rituals are quite ordinary, sometimes desirable, and often socially acceptable human tendencies. We get very necessary relief and enjoyment from them and they take many different forms in different cultures and societies. But when a person's self-harm moves from what is ordinarily acceptable, say from nail biting to cutting the skin on her tummy, acceptance is replaced with disgust or disapproval. We can also see piercings and tattooing as acts on this spectrum—they are acts which also speak of transgression, albeit that which is fashionably acceptable to some of us if not all of us. A small tattoo on the shoulder is one thing but tattoos all over the face, arms, legs, or knuckles reading "love and hate", elicit in others different degrees of emotional response. The "in your face/ on your face" tattoo or piercing draws the gaze of the Other, who can't but help look. This is an important part of the meaning of the act and is likely to connect to an original lack of attunement or mirroring in the individual's early experience. The person may be saying "Look at me" but may also be saying "Hate me as I hate myself/hate you for not seeing me well enough." It is a communication from the person concerned that he is unable to manage his emotional or psychological needs—in this case the need to be seen with love—without recourse to these actions; that he has insufficient internal resources to manage the world and the disappointments in it; that he needs help but fears the need for help lest it would be too much. This in turn can be a repetition of early failure in which as a baby he was experienced as too much by depressed or inadequate carers. The tattoo that reads "Love" says "Help", the one that reads "Hate" says "Go away." The tattoo or piercing that looks pretty says "Am I like this?"; the pain that it takes to put it there says something else.

To understand this further we need to appreciate the levels of dissociation or fragmentation in the person concerned. Our sense of reality and who we are depend on our being to a certain extent connected, in touch with, our feelings, thoughts, sensations, perceptions, and memories. If these become "disconnected" from each other, or don't register in our conscious mind, our sense of identity, our memories, and the way we see ourselves and the world around us will change. This is what happens when we dissociate. When we dissociate it is as if our mind has left our body and we are looking at ourselves from a distance.

Every one of us has periods when we feel disconnected. Sometimes this happens naturally and unconsciously. For example, we often drive a familiar route, and arrive with no memory of the journey or of what we were thinking about. But, importantly, we sometimes dissociate as a psychological defence mechanism to help us deal with, manage, and survive traumatic experiences either real or felt to be psychologically or emotionally threatening.

Dissociation makes the act of self-injury possible. People describing their own self-harm nearly always say that they do not feel pain, but this also makes the self-harm necessary. In other words, I dissociate because of unbearable heightened distress, overwhelming feelings that I cannot bear. I cut off and I cut. I feel cut off from feelings so I need to cut to feel something. The experience of physical contact, sensation, connects me up again to myself until the next time. As Turp says, "Self-harm emerges as a mode of self-handling and self-soothing, as a coping strategy that curtails unbearable states of mind by translating invisible internal damage into visible external damage and as an unconscious communication ..." (2003, p. 85). In this way self-harm is sometimes something like suicidality, but it can also, like depression, be a defence against suicide. If we think about suicide as an act of killing the mind off by killing the body—the aim being to stop unbearable psychic pain—then getting out of one's mind in other ways, by self-harming, begins to make some kind of sense. The excessive use and misuse of psychoactive illicit drugs and prescribed drugs are attempts to kill the mind *without* killing the body. Like depression, might taking drugs and drinking also be seen as defences against suicide or at least ways of coping with unbearable pain, and also ways of soothing the turmoil in and of the mind?

At this stage this may not be clear to some readers but I would hope that when we look further into the condition of the suicidal state of mind we can see both the differences and links between a suicidal act and self-harming activity described above. For the moment I want to emphasise the danger of linking them too closely together and of assuming that if someone self-harms he is necessarily suicidal. In fact the very opposite is more likely to be the case. This is an important cautionary note to those who are involved with working with people who self-harm since the desire and aims of treatment are often intended to stop the self-harm without realising that this might cause an escalation of the unbearable feelings, which may in turn lead to a more suicidal state. As Gardner states, people have quite strong responses to those who harm themselves: "… generally one of shock, fear, anger, disgust and revulsion which may lead to hostility and anxiety" (2001, p. 84). If we compare these feelings with those of the person involved we can see that they are in many ways the same. The shocking and painful quality of it all evokes the painful and unbearable experiences and emotions of the self-harming person. With the patient I described above, her self-harming continued through the first three and a half years of her therapy until she was able to relinquish the actions of harm to herself and work through her feelings and her internal conflicts with me in the therapy. None of this was easy or in some ways any less painful but because of the safety of the therapeutic relationship, and the capacity of the therapist to be a container of all the bad and confused feelings, it was no longer necessary to direct them into/against her body. Therapy with this patient continued for a number of years with no further actual self-injury to the body.

Self-harming is also often closely associated with previously experienced trauma. Trauma can be experienced, in Turp's words, as a kind of "piercing"—an intrusion into the person from someone or something outside, through the skin. This trauma, in cases of self-harming, is often literally physical. In the Bristol survey, out of the seventy-six women who were self-harming who took part, 46 per cent reported childhood sexual abuse and another 25 per cent physical abuse—acts of harm by another against the self but also acts of harm through the body. If we then think of the relationship of the self-harming act, often one of breaking through the skin, to the original trauma of sexual violation or beating, then the person is repeating it in both an attempt to heal and in an attempt to show. There is also here the bind described by Gardner. The "relationship" with the original abuser can "become internalised as an overwhelming, intrusive and dangerous figure in the psyche, yet one with whom there is a deep involvement, and from which it is hard to break free" (2001, p. 40). Sexual abuse is often perpetrated by a close "loved one" and it is explained to the child by the abuser as being special. This complete confusion of good with bad is psychologically devastating. The self-harming abused person then recreates this conflict and also the abuse by doing it to herself in many different ways. The scarring also manifests the poor, broken, hurt, fragile self/skin, but at the same time self-harmers toughen their skin/their selves by repeating the cutting or burning in the same place over and over again and in so doing hardening and toughening the skin. In this way the physical skin represents the psychic skin. This would also be in keeping with a need to keep adding additional tattoos and piercings to the body. Furthermore, research has shown that those who repeatedly self-harm increase their pain thresholds so that they have to increase the seriousness of the action. This need for greater pain can lead to suicide by "accident".

When we have had a good enough emotional and relational experience in early life we can bear our emotional wounds and let them heal. Just like our physical skin—good healthy skin will repair itself in time if it is broken. But when we have been pierced, traumatised physically, too often to be bearable, our psychic skin will be thin, leaky, or rigid and impervious. In this way we can understand self-harming symbolically and see that there is a dimension in it which is health seeking. Self-harm has the potential and perhaps the intention to relieve feelings of dissociation (of being cut off) to restore a feeling of normality and to stay in touch with life. In this way self-harmers may express a tendency "not to lose the psychosomatic linkage" (Winnicott, 1966, p. 113), not to "flip out". Reports of self-harm reveal this; they speak of gaining control, of the self-harm being "my way, my secret, something I do to make myself feel real". In contrast the suicidal person is seeking to escape, to not feel anything ever again. There is something much more dichotomous and completely split about this state of mind and we will explore this more fully in the following chapters. While the self-harmer holds onto the linkage the suicide tries to split it into two irretrievably. The suicide is breaking the psyche/soma linkage, using the body as the theatre on which to act it out with an intended finality, while the self-harmer is trying to keep the connection going. Suicide is not intended to be repeated. Self-harming is always about repetition even if in the end it may lead, by escalation or accident, to death.

Having made some distinction between self-harm and suicide, however, it is also important to alert ourselves to the dangerous overlap between the states. Those who have a persistent and enduring relationship to self-harm and self-injury are at higher risk of completed suicide. Recent research on what has been called "the acquired ability to enact lethal self-injury" (Thomas Joiner, in Joiner et al., 2009) suggests that the element of being able to face down the self-preservation instinct, to fly in the face of it, is a significant element in the ability to successfully kill oneself. Thus the capacity for suicide, it is proposed, can be exacerbated by repeated exposure to painful and also fearful experiences, which result in the person becoming habituated to the pain and increasingly able to tolerate pain, and which may ultimately lead to a dangerous fearlessness or carelessness in the face of death. In this theory, what is known as "acquired capability for suicide" is really a continuum, accumulating over time with repeated exposure to painful and provocative experiences conferring greater capacity for suicide. This is an interesting proposal and one which should alert us once more to the complexity of the human mind and behaviour. Those who self-harm may not in fact be suicidal but their increasing capacity to cause pain to themselves and then to become more inured to it, in and of itself, leads to a greater capacity for completed suicide.

In a direct test of acquired capability of suicide, Van Orden, Witte, Gordon, Bender, and Joiner (2008, pp. 72–83) showed that the number of past suicide attempts significantly predicted levels of acquired capability in a sample of outpatients. The highest levels of acquired capability were reported by individuals with multiple past attempts. Similarly, the model demonstrates that an increasing capacity for suicide is not limited just to prior suicide attempts but also to forms of repetitive pain and trauma, for example, repeated self-injury, self-starvation, physical abuse, etc. The likelihood of suicide attempts is greater in individuals who have a long history of self-injury, use a greater number of methods, and report absence of physical pain during self-harming or being harmed by others. This is certainly borne out by my experiences in the consulting room with patients who self-harm and who will describe having to increase the pain they inflict on themselves, or change from cutting to burning in order to be able to feel the pain they need to feel. As well as the habituation and tolerance that Joiner and colleagues describe, this also illustrates how growing despair and desperation mount when the method chosen to self-soothe no longer works.

So while it is important to differentiate between the suicidal condition and the various complex conditions of the mind that can lead to self-harm it is also necessary to be alert to the ways in which accelerating long-term self-injury, and an increasing failure to manage to "soothe", may lead to more deadly self-injury.

CHAPTER FOUR

Myths, misrepresentations, and fallacies

If we look at suicide historically, in a way it can be seen as a narrative of denouncement, suspicion, and opprobrium within the context of changing social and cultural norms. For the most part, suicide is either excused, appropriated, accounted for, or reviled within a number of prevailing orthodoxies—be they religious, political, cultural, or territorial. It is rarely simply allowed to be the human, individual experience that it is. It is more often misunderstood, misrepresented, and treated with great suspicion within wider society. It remains suspect. As such, there abound a great many competing pronouncements, explanations, theories, and excuses for suicide, historically and contemporaneously. They range from the sympathetic, the scientific, the sociological, the psychological, to the indignant and the dismissive. Many ideas about suicide contain part truths and part understandings. In Chapter Two we spent some time in the shark-infested waters of what is or is not a mental illness. Reducing suicidality to a mental illness is one such example of a part truth—it can be partly helpful, partly miss the point, and partly unhelpful. But there remain other fallacies and myths and responses to suicide which bear further examination in order that we may better understand what we are dealing with.

Perhaps many of the statements and pronouncements about suicide are made in order to make us feel more distant from our own connection with suicidality, to disavow ourselves from it almost completely. These accounts of suicide are made to keep suicide out there, entirely other than us, either by demarcating the suicidal as ill or disturbed, to be attended to in a medical model that will effectively diagnose them and then cure the problem, or as misguided, selfish, oppressed, misunderstood, or dangerous within a sociological, religious, cultural, criminal, or political framework. All these theories and models can take care of the problem of suicide without it getting too close to us. There is a really particular terror produced by suicide and a particular guilt—there but for the grace of God perhaps—because it is, actually, something we could all do and something which we can all feel drawn to or tantalised by. As Daniel Stern wrote: "… the failed lawyer, the cynical doctor, the depressed housewife, the angry teenager … all of mankind engaged in the massive conspiracy against their own lives that is their daily activity." Suicide smashes through any pretension we may have that life is easy—it reminds us all about our own part in the "massive conspiracy against our own lives". Consequently we are prone to fear it and set it apart.

In Europe within the Christian tradition suicide was denounced as a sin which was later embodied in law. Historical accounts of suicide depict instances of the bodies of people who have killed themselves being hanged; having stakes driven through their hearts like vampires; left at public marked sites—places of public execution. It is as if the suicidal person has acted out some kind of outrage and has to be publicly put down and degraded. And where religious condemnation was, then came criminality. There are baffling accounts from as late as nineteenth-century London, such as a man who having cut his own throat being brought back to life and then re-hanged for suicide! Laws remained in England in relation to the confiscation of the property of a suicide by the state until the late nineteenth century, and as late as 1961 an unsuccessful suicide could still be sentenced as having committed an unlawful act. In earlier times a person who took her own life would often be denied funeral rites or burial in a church cemetery. In practice, after the Enlightenment, once religious righteousness was challenged in the twentieth century the Church often showed sensitivity and weighed considerations of despair and mental health in favour of the suicide's need for forgiveness and understanding. Nowadays even the Catholic

Church concedes that the vast majority of suicides are consequences of an accumulation of psychological factors that impede making a free and deliberative act of will against God's gift of life. Catholic canon law now no longer specifically mentions suicide as an impediment to funeral rites or religious burial.

Scriptural pronouncements on suicide in the writings of the major world religions—Catholicism, Hinduism, Islam, Judaism, are mostly admonishments against taking your own life and couched either in the sanctity of life and the authority and mercy of God. The Quran states:

> And do not kill yourselves. Surely, God is Most Merciful to you. (4:29)
>
> And do not throw yourselves in destruction. (2:195)

Similarly the 1997 Catechism of the Catholic Church asserts:

> Everyone is responsible for his life before God who has given it to him. It is God who remains the sovereign Master of life. We are obliged to accept life gratefully and preserve it for his honour and the salvation of our souls. We are stewards, not owners, of the life God has entrusted to us. It is not ours to dispose of. (#2280)

In the Talmud (*Bava Kama* 91b), prohibition concerning suicide seems to be arrived at by a process of exegesis on the verse from the book of Genesis: "And surely your blood of your lives will I require" (9:5), interpreted as: "I will require your blood if you yourselves shed it." However, interpretations of the sixth commandment seem to imply that the prohibition of suicide is *not* felt to be contained in it. "Thou shalt not kill" (Exodus 20:13) is interpreted within both Jewish and Christian teachings to concern the act of murder, of killing another, but not the act of suicide, of killing oneself. And yet suicide *is* an act of killing. I wonder if the commandment is in fact intended to capture the possibility of both suicide and murder.

Hindu teachings on suicide are perhaps more complex in some ways. Suicide is largely regarded again as an act against life, which is regarded as sacred. Every creature has a unique responsibility to fulfil its life in its present incarnation. However, there were certain circumstances within the early ascetic traditions in which spiritually motivated suicide was permitted: selfiimmolation as an offering of the body to Fire (*Agni*);

death by slow starvation (*Prayopavesa*); making an offering of the body to Air—death by entering a cave and suspending breath in a state of self-absorption (*Samadhi*). Echoes of these more ancient ascetic practices remain today. Self-immolation—burning—is a much more common method of suicide in India than in other countries. Also the three methods of spiritual suicide are very close in some ways to modern forms of self-harm and self-injury—namely, burning, anorexia, and autoerotic asphyxiation. It occurs to me the religion's texts demonstrate age-old knowledge of the pull we may have towards death.

Such religious pronouncements and interpretations concerning suicide seem for the most part to contain prohibitions. There are exceptions, however. For example, martyrdom for one's religious beliefs, historically and contemporaneously, has been upheld within the Judaeo-Christian faith as well as the Muslim faith. But it is difficult to know the condition of the individual mind at work within the claim made that it is right to die for one's beliefs. Perhaps the fact that all religions do take a position in relation to suicide and to murder arises from a fundamental knowledge of how difficult it is to actually manage to live a life. How to live your life as well as you can is the territory of religious teaching after all. Religious doctrine appears to understand that extreme feeling and overwhelming emotions can give rise to extreme action. Hence religious teaching has something to say and observe about suicide even if the pronouncements do have a largely condemnatory feel.

Individual suicide, however, is largely a secular act, not carried out under a religious banner or in order to get to a better world. In fact the suicidal individual is more likely to be creating his own afterlife rather than trying to get into a ready-made heaven or sacred life beyond an earthly death. Research has shown that people "residing in nations with relatively high levels of religiosity, who are affiliated with one of four major faiths, are religiously committed, and are engaged with a religious network are found to be lower in suicide acceptability" (Stack & Kposowa, 2011, p. 289).

Today legal and religious punishments and condemnations on suicide that were once the norm have largely given way to more health orientated, psychological, sociological understandings about suicide, although we still use everyday language that associates suicide with criminality. Terms such as "committed suicide" are still commonly used. And in the UK and elsewhere suicides, regarded as they are as unexplained deaths, still require post-mortems and coroner's inquests to be held. A coroner's court is a legal setting with all the legal trappings that accompany such formal hearings—witnesses and experts have to give testimony, stand in a witness box, and are asked questions under oath by the coroner. The coroner gives a "verdict" on the cause of death. It's not the most sympathetic of arenas for the bereaved in their shock and bewilderment but it is the case that the censorious attitudes that once prevailed in law and religion have been superseded by more tolerant attitudes. However, I would argue that these more enlightened attitudes can be problematic and restrictive in quite different ways—namely in the way that we remove suicidality into the realm of mental illness and scientific explanation. This seems still to box suicide out of the way and emphasises the difficulty we have in allowing suicide to have its place as part of a very human state of mind. Prevalent current approaches and diagnoses attempt to reduce suicidality to a set of faulty behaviours, complex models of motivations and impulses, negative thoughts, or wrong genes. They deny or avoid the fact that suicide, as an act of killing, is underpinned by aggression turned against the self.

As well as statements which might be made in order to create distance, there are those which are genuine attempts at prevention. For professionals working with those who are suicidal—doctors, psychiatrists, mental health nurses, psychotherapists, counsellors, etc.—the aim is prevention. Ideas about prevention are often accompanied by attempts to map the mind, locate the suicidal point, and fix the person. For example, Professor Rory O'Connor, a health psychologist, currently head of the Suicidal Behaviour Research Laboratory (SBRL) at the University of Glasgow, is one of the UK's leading researchers into suicide and self-harm. The aim of this research is to apply theoretical models derived from different areas of psychology as well as from the social sciences to enhance understanding of self-harm and suicide. O'Connor and his team have produced a model which attempts to explain the suicidal trajectory. They call this "the integrated motivational–volitional model of suicidal behaviour" (IMV). In brief,

> The IMV proposes that suicidal behaviour results from a complex interplay of factors, the proximal predictor of which is one's intention to engage in suicidal behaviour. Intention, in turn, is determined by feelings of entrapment where suicidal behaviour is seen as the salient solution to life circumstances. These feelings of being trapped are triggered by defeat/humiliation appraisals,

which are often associated with chronic or acute stressors. The transitions from the defeat/humiliation stage to entrapment, from entrapment to suicidal ideation/intent, and from ideation/intent to suicidal behaviour are determined by stage-specific moderators (i.e., factors that facilitate/obstruct movement between stages). In addition, background factors (e.g., deprivation, vulnerabilities) and life events (e.g., relationship crisis), which comprise the premotivational phase (i.e., before the commencement of ideation formation) provide the broader biosocial context for suicide. (2011, p. 296)

Professor O'Connor goes on to emphasise his hope that this model can "delineate the different phases along the path to suicidal behaviour, which represent potential opportunities for intervention", stressing that "These ought to be explored in more detail, as through more targeted intervention, we will be better placed to prevent the experience of unbearable distress being translated into suicidal behaviour" (p. 297). Professor O'Connor is a man who himself has been touched by suicide through the death of a close friend, and his commitment to trying to further our understanding of suicide and his hope that his model can be used to help interventions is clearly well intentioned and comes from considerable neuroscientific and psychology research expertise. But I fear that such an elaboration, notwithstanding the skill and expertise involved, misses the heart of the matter almost completely. The professor names and articulates vividly the central features of the suicidal state: defeat, entrapment, constriction, etc., but describes this in such a way as to imply that were we somehow to invent an assessment algorithm that we could apply and "catch" people on the cycle we would then be able to intervene and stop the process. This is an admirable wish but can be an impediment in terms of helping those who are suicidal. Missing from this thinking are two very important aspects about suicide. One: that it is an unconscious act. Two: that it is an act of aggression. Yes, if the suicidal act is examined at face value, then the person's conscious acts, motivations, behaviours, etc. may well confirm the IMV model. However, the person is hell-bent on carrying out his intention because of how he feels about himself in relation to the world and vice versa *and* because of his dissociation from this feeling, namely from their unconscious aggression, which is not revealed by this or any other model. The intention is to kill the self and *at the same time aggress the Other.*

The real whammy in suicide, and what makes it so difficult to get hold of, is that, more often than not, the person does not know this herself. Usually her aggressive wishes are so deeply repressed, cut off, unknown, and, most important, felt to be unacceptable, that they are utterly repressed. There is alas no recognition of the unconscious in the professor's model. Of course it is understandable that we might want to search for an explanation about suicide—find a universally applicable theory. Theories can be a protection; they allow a form of non-attachment which we all need to survive such deaths, such full-blown attacks. But they also seduce us away from facing something and give us the lie that we can strike gold and find the algorithm that will predict a suicide and stop it entirely. We need to give ourselves more credit. These well-intentioned goals of prevention are often hindered if understanding does not come first. And understanding suicide is difficult and takes courage. It is ultimately an individual act born out of a need to kill the mind in order to torment another/end the anguish—this sort of understanding needs to come first and is crucial to any sort of prevention. We need first to find out about *this* anguish, *this* violent rage, *this* ambition, *this* triumph, in *this* person. The suicide is rejecting us so perhaps we reject her by refusing to understand and robbing her of the act's very meaning?

Another aspect which distorts our appreciation of suicide is the fact that official statistics on suicide reflect only a proportion of the real picture. For example, we might think that figures for suicide in the UK may be as much as twice the number currently given. Why should that be? Because sensitivity and prejudice have a hold on us in this area. Unwillingness to grasp the nettle of suicide leads to a lot of unintended and downright deliberate covering up. The car driven into a tree late one night—recorded as an accident; the drink and drug overdose recorded as "death by misadventure" and so on. For all sorts of good reasons and not so good reasons, unless there is unequivocal evidence—an unambiguous suicide note, clear evidence of lethal methods used, etc., coroners may not record a clear verdict of suicide but may hedge or prevaricate with either an open or a narrative verdict. Narrative verdicts, those that give an account of how an unexplained death occurred in a few descriptive sentences but do not make a clear pronouncement of any cause of death, are particularly tricky and are on the increase in the UK today. Many more inquests are ending in "narrative verdicts" rather than a ruling that someone killed themselves, often because of the coroner exercising caution. This means that many suicides go unrecorded as such, a statistic counterbalanced by the number of narrative verdicts rising from just 111 in 2001 to a staggering 3012 in 2009, so that the narrative verdict has become the outcome of more than one in ten inquest findings. This is despite the fact that suicide is sometimes strongly implied in the verdict. The trouble with this is manifold. By masking the real numbers in this way it could affect how we evaluate current national suicide prevention programmes—are suicide rates in fact falling in the UK as the strategists claim?—and also how seriously we respond to suicide. Also, because coroners vary greatly in their use of narrative verdicts, suicide rates may seem to decline in areas served by coroners who favour reaching such verdicts.

Narrative verdicts are not in themselves the culprit; they are but the next in line from what previously were verdicts of accident or misadventure. But what their increasing use indicates is how widespread and ongoing is our collective wish to disguise suicide. Is this perhaps due in some part to an unconscious wish to deny the suicide a successful attack on us, as well as to the more obvious, and in my opinion mistaken, sensitivity to the bereaved, or also to possible political duplicity?

The World Health Organization is extremely well placed to talk about suicide and has some excellent material available. Among its recent publications, which include *Preventing Suicide: A Global Imperative*, you can find a document which is called simply "Myths". It is interesting to me that the WHO felt impelled to create this list of myths and rebuttals since it bears out the idea that we remain compelled to repudiate suicide and distance ourselves from it in many ways. The following are some of the myths identified and debunked by the WHO:

Myth: *Once someone is suicidal, he or she will always remain suicidal.*
  Fact: Heightened suicide risk is often short term and situation-specific. While suicidal thoughts may return, they are not permanent and an individual with previously suicidal thoughts and attempts can go on to live a long life.

Myth: *Talking about suicide is a bad idea and can be interpreted as encouragement.*
  Fact: Given the widespread stigma around suicide, most people who are contemplating suicide do not know who to speak to. Rather than encouraging suicidal behaviour, talking openly can give an individual other options or the time to rethink his/her decision, thereby preventing suicide.

Myth: Only people with mental disorders are suicidal.

Fact: Suicidal behaviour indicates deep unhappiness but not necessarily mental disorder. Many people living with mental disorders are not affected by suicidal behaviour, and not all people who take their own lives have a mental disorder.

Myth: Most suicides happen suddenly without warning.

Fact: The majority of suicides have been preceded by warning signs, whether verbal or behavioural. Of course there are some suicides that occur without warning. But it is important to understand what the warning signs are and look out for them.

Myth: Someone who is suicidal is determined to die.

Fact: On the contrary, suicidal people are often ambivalent about living or dying. Someone may act impulsively by drinking pesticides, for instance, and die a few days later, even though he would have liked to live on. Access to emotional support at the right time can prevent suicide.

Myth: People who talk about suicide do not mean to do it.

Fact: People who talk about suicide may be reaching out for help or support. A significant number of people contemplating suicide are experiencing anxiety, depression, and hopelessness and may feel that there is no other option.

I would add to this two other commonly held beliefs which we often hear spoken:

Myth: If someone survives suicide they are no longer a risk.

Myth: Once a person has tried suicide they will not try again.

Fact: Having tried and not completed a suicide a person can remain at very high risk. The fact of "failing" may well reinforce feelings of worthlessness and uselessness and lead to a greater suicidality. It is important to take seriously their intention to kill themselves and not disregard it because it has not succeeded. A cautionary note too—it is not good practice to assess the seriousness of the suicidal intention by the unsuccessful method. Just because a person did not manage to kill themselves by, say, not taking a sufficiently toxic dose of medication, or jumping from a window that is not at a lethal height, this does not indicate a lack of seriousness or intention. However, it is also the case that some people judge the lethality of the toxic medication quite knowingly in order to create a cry for help. As these contradictions demonstrate nothing is quite what it seems in regard to suicidality.

So this is a useful list which speaks for itself. But I would draw particular and urgent attention to that most prevalent of myths, namely, that if we talk about suicide to someone we will give him the idea and put dangerous ideas into his head. This is absolutely not the case. If a person is a suicidal it is a great relief to be able to talk about it and to realise that someone else can bear it. This of itself is therapeutic and may even be enough to move that person from immediate danger. One of the horrendous features of suicide is isolation, becoming withdrawn from the world. Once someone has asked the person about suicide, and is prepared to listen to her, this very dangerous aspect of suicide, feeling utterly on her own with it, has already shifted. On the other hand, if she is not suicidal and she is asked about it there is no harm done. It may even help her formulate better what she is feeling and what state of mind she is in. It may be a relief for her to realise she is not suicidal.

One of the reasons that we do not easily enter the territory of suicide with another is our fear—fear of what she might say and a fear that we will not know how to respond, together with a sense that we will have to do something about it. Another possible reason for avoiding talking with someone who is suicidal, or with someone who you think might be, is a sort of embarrassment. As if, like talking about death itself, it is not the thing we do, not quite respectable, not quite right. It can only be done sotto voce, in a coded or secretive way, or not at all. As if we are sparing the blushes of the suicidal person or our own! But as the WHO document points out, talking openly, even if you are not a professional, can relieve the pressure and open up options that the person can follow up with your support. Once someone is talking there is really very little you have to do except listen in the first instance. The Samaritans are particularly good in this way. All their training focuses on helping volunteers to speak clearly and openly about suicide with those callers who are suicidal.

There are also other myths I would add to the WHO list, some more important than others. It is often felt that bad weather and long dark winter nights contribute to rises in suicide. But actually the evidence is to the contrary. Suicide rates appear to peak in the spring and summer and actually fall off in late autumn, although Christmas often brings its own pressures. This seems perfectly understandable to me. Just when all around starts springing into life, the weather starts to improve, the buds burst, etc., the suicidal and depressed feel all the more frozen, left out in the cold, in contrast to the liveliness around them. It makes you hate life even more when you see it going on all around you. At least in winter everyone retreats a bit. Spring and summer may well accentuate the feelings of isolation, remove, and despair in the suicidal mind.

Another misrepresentation about suicide, which was touched on in Chapter One, is that it is a young person's tragedy. Not so. To be sure, young people are a high-risk group but that is largely to do with their overall rate of death being so low. It is also to do with their lack of experience of coping and surviving the challenges of life. As we get older most of us have faced some difficulties in our time and can hold onto the idea that things will improve. We have also accrued the resources to help or get help for ourselves. Yes, young people attempt suicide in significant numbers, probably higher than other age groups. But completed suicides are more common in older people. Today men aged 35–49 are now the group with the highest suicide rate in the UK with people over seventy also having significantly high rates of death by suicide. Perhaps this flags up another myth—that of the peace and serenity of old age.

There are also often quoted references to geographical and national differences in suicidality. The implication seems to be that some countries are more suicidal than others. According to Alvarez (1971), in the eighteenth century England was known as a veritable hotbed of suicide. Nowadays we seem to think the Swedes or Finns head the suicide league table. But any notion that certain countries have significantly more suicides than others is so muddied by cultural, religious, and bureaucratic differences when it comes to collecting data that it is risky to draw any conclusions about national character when it comes to suicidality. The WHO does publish suicide rates worldwide and they are very wide-ranging with Guyana registering seventy per 100,000 male deaths in 2014 compared to two per 100,000 in Jamaica. The UK comes out lower than most European countries at twelve per 100,000 for both men and women combined. Personally I would be wary about drawing too many conclusions about national character from these statistics, although certainly conditions in the country and access to lethal methods will play a very significant part in these differing rates. For example, suicide rates in India and other parts of Asia have gone up considerably since the introduction of toxic pesticides made them available to often impoverished rural farmers. This seems to illustrate the dangerous connection between perturbation, impulsivity, and access to lethal means that can result in such increased rates of suicide.

However, while we are on this subject it might be worth adding here a note about Japan, a country which historically and culturally has had a very particular relationship to suicide. Japanese society's attitude towards suicide has had a sort of cultural tolerance, which stems from the historical function of suicide in battle. In feudal Japan, honourable suicide among Samurai (Japanese warriors) was considered a justified response to failure or inevitable defeat in battle. Traditionally, *seppuku* involved the slashing open of one's stomach with a sword. The purpose of this was to release the Samurai's spirit upon the enemy and thus avoid dishonourable execution at the hand of an enemy. There are other complications to do with how the self is regarded in Japan. For the Japanese, acceptance and conformity are valued above one's individuality. As a result of this it may be that in Japan one's self-worth is more strongly associated with how one is perceived by others. After the Second World War, Emperor Hirohito took the unprecedented step of broadcasting on national radio a plea to the nation to accept surrender, in other words not to choose to die honourably having lost the battle. He ordered his subjects to continue to live. This historical notion of suicide as a noble tradition still has some resonance in Japan today. In 2007 a cabinet minister, Toshikatsu Matsuoka took his life while being investigated in an expenses scandal. The former governor of Tokyo, Shintaro Ishihara, described him as a "true Samurai" for preserving his honour. Although Japanese culture historically permitted more tolerant views on the morality and social acceptability of suicide, there are indications that there is increasing public concern about suicide now and that attitudes are changing in modern Japan. In particular, the trend of increased internet usage among adolescents and young adults as well as the rising popularity of websites related to suicide has raised concerns in Japan about group suicides which appear to be organised online. We will return to a more detailed discussion on group and copycat suicides in later chapters.

Finally, I want to touch on the differing rates of suicide among certain jobs and professions—namely, that there are certain professions that have higher rates of suicide than others. In the USA and until recently in the UK, doctors, dentists, vets, and farmers were all rated as very high-risk groups for suicide. But it is important to note that while people in these jobs may experience high stress levels, possible increased isolation, and also a predisposition not to ask for help, the overarching reason for these professions being so deadly is that they all have access to lethal means and the knowledge that goes with them. If a doctor or vet is suicidal he or she is unlikely to make a mistake in a self-administered lethal dose of drugs. Hence any suicide attempt in these groups is very likely to be completed. It may be too speculative to think too much about the conditions that arise within the profession itself that might cause suicide. Rather it is more helpful to concentrate on the safe keeping of medicines and guns as well as raising awareness among these professional groups as to the need to ask for help at an early stage. In fact there is every indication in the UK that rates are declining for several of these groups, perhaps because of heightened awareness. These days, higher numbers are seen among manual occupations such as construction workers and plant/machine operatives (Roberts, Jaremin, & Lloyd, 2013, p. 6). This may be connected with employment uncertainty and low income more than access to lethal means. As with most data any reasoning about occupations and their link to suicide rates is difficult to confirm. There are as we know multiple factors which abound in suicide. Along with accessibility to suicide methods, competitiveness, perfectionism, and with it the real or perceived demands of others, instability in the job market and the consequent feeling of lack of control, may also be contributing factors in making certain occupations more vulnerable to suicidality. Jobs such as farming which are at the mercy of external factors such as the weather can make a person feel out of control. In occupations such as medicine, dentistry, pharmacy, and the law, wherein the threat of malpractice is extremely high, particularly in the USA, rates of suicide remain high. Other jobs may require long or antisocial working hours, causing isolation and difficulties in social interaction. Again, an example would be the farmer who spends all day working by him- or herself, maybe only occasionally interacting with others while carrying a lot of financial and other responsibility. But a cautionary note is needed when considering all these variables—even if we could agree that doctors have higher than average rates of suicide when compared to other professions this does not confirm that it is the requirements of the job itself that cause the suicidality. It is possible that along with all the variables cited above the type of person drawn to the profession may have a high degree of perfectionism and issues with competitiveness and control. Suffice to say there is evidence that some occupations have higher rates of suicide, and it is as well to be forewarned. Here in the UK work has been done by various professional bodies representing medicine and veterinary science to counter this, and the trend seems to show this is helping reduce rates in these professions. But it would be far too simplistic to conclude that it is just the jobs themselves that do the damage.

In conclusion, I think it is significant that there are, and have always been, so many myths, superstitions, fallacies, prohibitions, and mis-representations about suicide throughout history and across the globe. These are so strong that an organisation as prominent as the WHO must publish a list to debunk those still held with such tenacity today. Perhaps this is so because we need to reject suicide so emphatically. As Alvarez says: "In the end the suicide is rejected because he is so completely rejecting. All the traditional fallacies are ways of denying his sour Pyrrhic victory and robbing it of meaning" (1971, p. 108). Is it that each myth or misrepresentation is a way of devaluing the act of the suicidal person because we are at some level so angry that the lives of those of us left behind, those of us who live on, have been so utterly and completely rejected? Winnicott, in speaking of how the psychoanalyst might feel about his or her patients, wrote: "However much (he) loves his patients (he) cannot avoid hating them and fearing them, and the better (he) knows this the less hate and fear will be the motives in deter-mining what (he) does to his patients" (1947, p. 195). In the same way I think the better we know about our hate and fear of the suicide the less hate and fear will determine how we try to sort them out. Misun-derstanding is a form of rejection—"I just don't (want to) get it." But the paradox is that by "getting it", allowing it, rather than misunderstand-ing or dismissing it or modelling it, we are likely to do far more good and are more likely to prevent suicide. In a way this is a fundamental inversion which contrasts with that of the suicidal person who cannot tolerate much about himself and the world and decides therefore to reject it completely.

CHAPTER FIVE

The suicidal condition

In the introductory chapters we have examined some of the ideas, common constructs, understandings, and misunderstandings about suicidality. Now we will look further into the condition of the suicidal mind and examine it in some depth. The hope is that we may then have both a better understanding of this condition and also perhaps be relieved of some of the terror, rejection, guilt, or disdain, or other strong feelings, that may arise when we are asked to think about suicide. That which is able to be faced is better able to be accepted than that which is not. To accept that the condition of suicide might always be with us as part of the human struggle is not the same as ignoring it with a phlegmatic/dismissive "People kill themselves so we should just let them", nor is it the same as trying to stop it happening, but rather it is about our decision and our ability to tolerate it. This of itself is a helpful act, perhaps the most helpful act in relation to the suicidal person: for us to try to tolerate what the suicidal person believes cannot be tolerated by them or about them.

So we know that suicide is strongly linked to depression, to malignant sadness, to hopelessness, to despair, and, most important of all, to loss. The suicidal person feels that life is not worth living and that death is preferable. As Shneidman emphasises, death is felt to be "the *only* way", implying as this does the deadly impasse of the wished-for life that the person does not have, versus the necessary death. Whereas pessimism, depression, hopelessness are very important emotional states and are often present in a suicidal condition, they are only half the story. If we are to understand suicide and be more effective in helping those who are suicidal we also have to be very aware of the aggression and the violence behind the suicidal act, and behind suicidal thinking. Suicide is most definitely linked to violence. The suicidal act is a violent act of killing someone and killing is different from dying. Both terms refer to the fact that the individual has stopped living, that death has occurred. It's the manner in which this event has happened that differentiates the meaning of the two words. "Killed" suggests that the death was not due to natural causes, but by some external agency. When we say that someone has "died", we are indicating that the individual's death was due to natural causes: no one was the cause of his or her death.

Let us return to Stekel's statement: "No one kills himself who has never wanted to kill another or at least wished the death of another." In this statement Stekel articulates the anger and violence *against the Other* inherent in the suicidal act. The punishment which the person inflicts on him- or herself, albeit not necessarily consciously felt to be punishment, is punishment of A. N. Other, or every Other, the Other who is felt to be the cause of the suffering. It is often deceptively and unconsciously concealed, disguised, and turned into something very different: as self-sacrifice, or self-punishment, or self-loathing. The person who is despairing of themselves is actually despairing of the world. I remember one suicidal patient saying: "If I kill myself people will think I am selfish so I want to make it look like an accident; if I kill myself it'll look like I have only thought of myself and not how it may make other people feel." Actually what she was saying was the reverse of this: "I want to be so selfish and I want other people to feel really bad about my death. I cannot in life be as selfish as I need to be, as I have never been able to be. I want to be able to *not* care about other people so that I can be cared for enough. I want to be the baby I needed to be." She, and other suicidal people, are not accusing themselves but are accusing some lost loved one or an idea of the never had loved one, the lost Other who at one time very early on provided everything or should have provided everything—someone who "changed our misery into bliss, as if by magic" (Phillips, 2012, p. 10) when we could not do it ourselves.

This is often a never had loved one—the Other who did not quite provide enough of what was needed when it was necessary.

And here we are guided to another crucial element in the suicidal
complex, namely the notion of loss and thwart. It is as if the suicidal
person has suffered such a loss, either actual or perceived, from which
they are not willing or able to recover. I deliberately draw a distinction
here between the phrases "not willing" and "not able". These terms
have neither the same meaning nor quite the same purpose. When I
talk of "not willing to" I am implying a kind of defiance/obstinacy, an
angry determination not to accept the loss. When I talk of "not able to"
I am thinking more of a state of unpreparedness, as if in some devel-
opmental way the person cannot face loss, does not know how to deal
with it. Both states may be true and the two states are not mutually
exclusive. The important point is the angry disavowal of the loss. In his
book *Missing Out*, Adam Phillips talks not only of the difficulty we have
with frustration and with change, but also of our difficulty with being
responsible for change. Quoting Stanley Cavell on *King Lear* in his book
Discovering Knowledge (2003), he writes: "'We would rather murder the
world than permit it to expose us to change.' We would rather destroy
everything than let other people change us, so strong is our memory
of how changed we were at the beginning of our lives by certain other
people" (2012, p. 10). We are always seeking ways to resist change and
to refuse frustration. In this way it is as if at some level we resist change
so much that our very lives depend on not changing, or to put it another
way, with suicide, our very death depends on refusing to change. To
survive and live inevitably involves multiple grievous losses—whereas
killing oneself puts an end to suffering the pain of loss and the inevitability of more loss.

So how does this aggressive attack on the world transform into suicidality? In the more defiant position there is a more conscious anger,
which I think is linked to a different form of suicidal acting out by comparison with the more hapless giving up of the "not able" state. Either
way in the suicidal state the body of the suicidal person is treated as
a separate object and in so doing the aggressive feelings that are the
result of unprocessed historical felt or real losses which have become so
impossible to tolerate are inflicted on the individual's body. The mind
becomes divided due to this unbearable state: "If I destroy these feelings I will have rid myself of them, but if I don't destroy these feelings

I will continue to be faced with this devastating loss that I cannot bear. So I turn it against myself—it is me who is bad and destructive for having these thoughts, so I'll get rid of me." This kills (literally) two birds with one very lethal stone. "I will kill the body of myself in order to keep my mind intact and also destroy the Other through my murderous act." As Freud stated: "It is this *sadism* alone that solves the riddle of the tendency to suicide which makes melancholia so interesting and so dangerous … the ego can kill itself only if … it can treat itself as an object—if it is able to direct against itself the hostility which relates to an object and which represents the ego's original reaction to objects in the external world" (1917e, p. 252). (The use of the word "object" here is a particular usage in psychoanalytic discourse and can be confusing. It actually refers to another person, in effect another person to whom we were/are in relationship (for example our mother and father) and who we internalise. We then behave towards the world in certain ways because of these significant psychological relations, which are known as object relations in psychoanalytic parlance.)

We all experience loss, and to go back to Phillips what comes with loss is a requirement and a resistance to change, to accept that change has occurred with the loss. In the suicidal condition we capture the real enormity of what is required to manage loss and change, and how frail, faulty, and furious is our capability in doing so. Melanie Klein, the psychoanalyst, following on from but also disagreeing with Freud's thinking, took the idea of loss and how we experience it further, arguing (1963) that losing someone revives all earlier losses which as a baby are attributed to one's own destructiveness. The baby, in order to survive his very primitive hate of the mother who goes away when for example feeding is finished, feels bad himself in order to preserve the object/mother that he needs to keep good. Later, if someone close to us is lost to us, we may often feel responsible for the loss—we may even feel consciously that we wished for that person to go/die because we had mixed feelings about them. What is so important about Klein's work was how she emphasised the ambivalent nature of our relationships to others, whom we can both love and hate at the same time. It is developmentally important to be able to work through what Klein termed the psychological mechanism of splitting—keeping the bad and good apart—so that we are in time able to integrate the bad and the good, to bring them together and to realise that we can love and hate the same person, that that person may be both good and bad as are we ourselves.

An important development of sorrow, concern, and reparation follows this mental achievement, which Klein termed achieving the depressive position. The implication of this thinking is that if early natural struggles around the loss of the wholly good mother are not dealt with properly, in other words if the child is not able to properly rage and hate with relative ease, depressive illness is more likely to ensue and with it self-hate and self-blame. Klein's thinking helps us understand both the hate and the polarisation experienced in the suicidal position—here we find a regression back to splitting (the world is bad, I am good or the world is good and I am bad, both equally totalitarian and constricted, convincing reasons to exit stage left). The almost complete split-off rage/hate and the constriction of thinking demonstrates an absence at the moment of suicidality of a capacity for concern and compassion for either oneself or for the Other.

Klein's thinking also helps us to see why, given that death, the ultimate loss, is very clearly known to us, it is remarkably difficult for us to accept. All sorts of external events can be felt by us to be like a loss and also deeply personal. Each loss revives earlier losses and revives one's hatred, and if we take this further, a hatred of one's hatred—in other words self-reproach—a very suicidal phenomenon. The end of an affair, the result of an exam, the shape of our bodies, the latest sales figures, the number of Facebook friends—these are all arenas for loss to be felt, any of which can easily be believed to be a consequence of rejection or thwart. Klein's ideas make sense of how and why we are so very susceptible to turning painful experiences into personal failures or injuries when they may well be examples of an everyday story of everyday folk. We are all to some extent narcissists. We seem to crave explanations for the events that affect us and our lives as if somehow we could rid ourselves of them by making them our own or someone else's fault. Suicide is the most extreme version of this narcissistic reasoning and it becomes a justification, once arrived at, from which it is very hard to return.

In suicide the act or the idea of the act of suicide seems often to revolve around a notion of settling scores. These scores may not even be very clear, and certainly not conscious. But there is such a strong sense of grievance that the person has been utterly and unfairly thwarted, a feeling which seems to go right back to early childhood. In *The Silent Woman*, Janet Malcolm's biography of the poet Sylvia Plath who killed herself in 1963, Malcolm reflects on an account related to her by Olwyn Hughes, Plath's sister-in-law. This concerned a confrontation between

Plath and Hughes at the family house in Yorkshire after which Plath stole off at dawn the next day without a word leaving Olwyn to wonder why Plath didn't say anything:

> Below the surface of Olwyn's story of the Yorkshire confrontation with its score settling atmosphere lie deep wounds, and one of them is surely the wound from which survivors of suicide never recover. Plath, as we know, left at dawn on another day in 1963. The suicide goes away and the survivors are forever in the wrong. They are like the damned who can never make amends, who have no prospect of grace. Olwyn's "Why didn't she say something?" expresses the anguish and anger of those who have been left without a word in a lake of fire. (1995, p. 196)

This vignette illustrates so powerfully how the suicide leaves no possibility of mutual reparation. The sense of blame is palpable. The poet John Berryman also makes painfully clear this connection between the suicidal person's rage and the aftermath felt by the survivor in his poem *Dream Song 235*: "Save us from shotguns & fathers' suicides … do not pull the trigger or all my life I'll suffer from your anger killing what you began" (1968, p. 164). Berryman's father shot himself when Berryman was twelve years old. John Berryman killed himself in 1972.

Of course it is the case that many suicides occur in adults who appear to have had an averagely normal sort of childhood but then seem not to have been able to bear loss or trauma in adulthood—the loss of a partner, job, reputation. I am inclined to think that the difficulty in not being able to survive or endure these adult difficulties, immensely hard as they can often be, does lie in the subsoil of the personality laid down in childhood even if this is not evident at the time. Shneidman puts this well:

> Suicide never stems from happiness—it happens because of the stark absence of it. In relation to suicide genuine happiness has an almost magical aura to it. Or to put it another way unhappiness reflects the lost joys of an unrealised childhood. Early childhood is the time when we can—unrestrained by realistic and adult rule and actualities—fantasise about what we would optimally like to have happen within ourselves and between ourselves and our parents. (1996, p. 163)

In childhood our imagination needs to come into being, come alive, be encouraged, so we can create stories, narratives, fantasies, and whole worlds within our play. All these childhood experiences become, if allowed to develop, essential in managing the vicissitudes of the real world both in childhood and forever after. But if we don't have the conditions for this important experience in childhood, or if we have it and it is taken from us, it is as if the cut is too deep and the scars too long held and never healed. To quote Shneidman again:

> It is not possible to be robbed totally of one's childhood but what does happen can seem to be just as bad ... Perhaps every person who commits suicide *at any age* has been a victim of a vandalised childhood in which the preadolescent child has been psychologically mugged or sacked, and has had psychological needs, important to *that* child, trampled on and frustrated by malicious preoccupied adults, or obtuse adults. I tend to believe at rock bottom, the pains that drive suicide relate primarily not to the precipitous absence of equanimity or happiness in adult life but to the haunting losses of childhood's special joys. (1996, p. 164)

I love this thinking. To me it captures so much the sense of grievance and thwart that I frequently encounter when I talk to suicidal people. Yes, there are often immediate and pressing problems that cause people to think "now is the winter of my discontent". But behind this, in the fabric of the tale they tell is a constant underlying low level keening. It has the feel of a cry not so much of despair but more like "It's not fair, it should not have been like this." There can be a palpable sense of the unwillingness to endure pain or even to have to have it in the first place. "Why me? Why not them?" It is as if they cannot accept their pain—it does not fit their idea of what their lives should be like. They may have been given an idealised perfectionist view of the lives they should live, which is to say they have not been given a real sense of themselves, or they have been given very little sense of care and love as a child. I agree, along with other analysts like Shneidman, that one of the long-range aims in any therapeutic treatment of the suicidal, incredibly difficult as it will be given that the psychic state is so precarious, is to help those who are suicidal to change their concept of themselves. Only then do they stand some chance of truly acknowledging what might be terrible pain and simultaneously appreciating firstly, that this pain is not unique to them, and secondly that it is not in fact radically different from anyone's pain, and lastly that it is also pain that anyone could expect to have in life.

Shit happens. It happens to us all. However, with suicidal people you get the impression that they feel that their pain is somehow greater, unendurable, special—it borders on grandiosity. I think this connects with Phillips's point above, about a refusal to compromise and about the anger towards an Other, a fury towards the world which seems to be trying to make them change. The suicidal are refusing to have a relationship to all that is in the world, good and bad, and talking only to themselves. And the dialogue at this point can be fairly self-obsessed or narcissistic.

At this point I am reminded very starkly of my sister and her death. As we grew up it was as if Olivia held a very fragile preoccupied place in the family. It was she who tried to claim and hang on to the idea of childhood that Shneidman describes above in ways that the rest of us did not. She had a lovely imagination. In the face of some pretty wretched family experiences she went into herself, she was artistic, she drew, she wrote poetry, she dreamed of being an actor. These expressions of hers were often ridiculed or dismissed by parts of the family at the time—she was the butt of dismissive jokes and some brutal shaming. Thinking about the seeds of suicidality as stemming from thwarted childhood needs, Olivia was certainly thwarted in her claim, her ambition, to have the childhood she needed. A fanciful, magical childhood of dreams, of consuming inventiveness. I am thinking of Shneidman's emphasis above—"The preadolescent child ... has had psychological needs important to *that* child trampled on ..." It is the use of the term "*that child*" that sticks out now for me. For Olivia, perhaps because of her innate personality, her creative capability, or because of her position in the family, arriving a few years after a much heralded brother and a pretty, clever sister, and then having only a few months before I was conceived, the need to have her special joys nourished was overwhelming but sadly much traduced. When I think of it now she did her best— she had my father on side which I think helped. He was an artistic and gentle man but very passive in relation to our mother. He tried to help her with her various creative interests as much as he could but this was only very limited in scope and always against the backdrop of an uncontainable, collapsing, demanding spouse and four other children! I remember I felt very pulled into her needs and demands, not realising at all how significant this was, but at some level certainly grasping some-thing about the quality of her neediness which I can remember made me feel scared—with hindsight I would use the word overwhelmed. We spent hours together composing songs, putting on musicals, making up stories, playing fantasy games, but I was generally the gofer, the back room girl. Little did I realise what Olivia was *actually* doing, and why, in using her imagination so manifestly, she was attempting to have a wished-for life as opposed to the real life with which she was struggling.

Throughout these years I was always preoccupied, worried that things would fall apart with some dreadful sense of foreboding. And then my father died—and I think that this terrible loss cemented the sense of betrayal that had dogged Olivia's early years and that haunted her until she killed herself some ten years after his death. One other thing I do remember, which scared and puzzled me at the time, is that Olivia took to wandering at night time. She and I always shared a bedroom and from about the age of fourteen she would regularly get up in the middle of the night and go out. I would lie there and wait, worried sick, until she came back. When I asked her where she went she would snap and tell me to stop fussing, or just say "I just walk around, sometimes I go to xxxxxxx Common." This did nothing to reassure me and I don't think it was supposed to, but strangely, sadly, I never told anyone—I think by then I did not trust either parent to help and it did not occur to me that anyone else would. Maybe I also unconsciously wished her gone? After all I was an envious, thwarted child too, and her needs were very preoccupying! With hindsight I can think of this now as both the beginning of a very severe depression for Olivia which lasted really until she died but also as a period when she was searching, and also wanting very much to be found.

Using this example it is important to recognise that the individual may have no real idea of where these wounds, this haunting sense of loss, have come from—why she feels so aggrieved even though the wounded feelings are more often palpable and lifelong. When given the opportunity, many suicidal people talk of this—of always having had such feelings as far back as they can remember. The injured, thwarted, and rejected child they felt themselves to be is transformed over time into the psychologically disabled adult doomed for ever to feel injured, thwarted, and rejected. The wounds of their past will not heal over like they do for the rest of us. I think this is a kind of repudiation but not a conscious one. It is as if any good that comes in the present does little or nothing to modify this haunting sense of grievance. In contrast, for those of us who have had enough solid, early, sensitive, and sensible, consistent, good enough love, we are able to compromise, to take the rough with the smooth, to allow good experiences to reverberate and remain in our minds at the expense of bad experiences which we can manage and allow to fade.

Freud referred to these sorts of grievances as ghosts which haunt us: "That which cannot be understood inevitably reappears; like an unlaid ghost that cannot rest until the mystery has been solved and the spell broken" (1909b, p. 122). I think Olivia's wanderings were a way of repeatedly trying to find something, someone, looking, and repeating. We can see suicide in this way as an end to the wandering, the haunting. The trouble with suicide is that as a solution to the so-called mystery it is absolutely final and absolutely destructive. One of the many tragic aspects of adult suicide, when we think of it like this, is that those in the immediate firing line—the spouse, children, parents, close friends, and colleagues—suffer the full force of the aggressive destructive power—but like the person involved they have no idea, and, what is more important, no connection, to its origin. Even parents—who heaven knows must surely go through indescribable horror if their child kills him- or herself—may have little or no knowledge or understanding of the battles that their child felt utterly compelled to live and die by. All this time the poisonous, destructive rage has been working its insidious way to the surface, based on unknown losses, grievances, and injuries so sorely felt and retained unconsciously from way back, but cleverly disguised and defended under all sorts of tricks, masks, behaviours, guises, and character traits—perfectionism, martyrdom, rescuing, sadism, masochism, risk taking, false persona, passive aggression, helplessness, bullying, arrogance, lying, stealing, drug taking, alcohol, promiscuity, self-injury—the list is exhaustive!

One useful way into revealing the painful mystery of suicidality is by viewing the suicidal act as a sort of catastrophic expression of the type of conflict to which that particular person felt wedded and from which they were ultimately unable to deviate. In other words each suicide is actually a posthumous communication about that person's unconscious. If we are able to examine the fantasy behind the suicidal act, which is one of the potentials of psychotherapeutic treatment, we can know much more about the unconscious meaning of the suicidal act, and hopefully be able to reduce the imperative of the action. We will look in more detail at the types of suicidal fantasy in the next chapter.

But for now let us look more closely at the condition of the mind of the person in the grip of suicidal thinking. One of the main characteristics of the suicidal state of mind, which most professionals from all persuasions will agree on, is that of *constriction*—the narrowing of focus, an almost complete tunnel vision. It is as if the person has closed down, shut off all contact with the outside world, with all other possibilities, and reduced attention to a completely binary position—"the wished-for life I cannot have versus the necessary death, life as I want it as it must be or not at all—my way or the highway"! And at the time of suicide the necessary death is the *only* option. Shneidman talks of the word "only" as being the most dangerous word in the suicidal lexicon and I can see why. This simple word when used by someone who is expressing suicidal thoughts is such a stark indicator of this particularly lethal, all or nothing, dichotomous thinking. Alvarez describes this so well: "Once a man decides to take his own life he enters a shut off, impregnable but wholly convincing world where every detail fits and every incident reinforces his decision. Each of these deaths has its own inner logic and unrepeatable despair" (1971, p. 144). But the trouble with the logic of the suicide is that it is too simple, too convincing, too unreal. It is a black and white film; there is no colour, no nuance, no variation, and no dynamic. There is such an element of totality about it. Sometimes when I listen to suicidal people I am very struck by this. How convincing and convinced they sound—you can find yourself being persuaded so skilful and rehearsed are their arguments! But this logic is queer. It is not like any other kind of reasoning—as Alvarez says, "It is the unanswerable logic of a nightmare" (1971, p. 144).

The other important condition of mental life to be considered when looking more closely at the suicidal state of mind is that of *ambivalence*. Listening to a person who is expressing a suicidal intention, an intention to act on suicide, we are actually listening to a person expressing two distinct and almost completely separate aims: a conscious aim—the aim to die and end the misery/failure/despair that is being expressed, and the unconscious aim—the aim to survive! The person who talks of suicide is actually talking to you about a wish to live; or more accurately about the part of themselves that wishes to live.

Now this may sound odd to readers who may not be so familiar with the territory of the unconscious but it is at the time of this precarious suicidal state that the wish to die coexists with the wish to live. The person deludes himself that he will somehow go on in order to appreciate the satisfaction of the suicidal act. He imagines that some part of him will continue to live on, the mind perhaps, in some state so that he benefits from the solution he is about to inflict on himself. To paraphrase Freud, when the person reaches the point at which he intends to kill himself, he experiences the body as a separate object. It is as if at this point there is a delusional aspect to the state of mind—I am not meaning that all suicidal people are mad, not at all, but in order for it to make sense to them there is an almost complete separation of the body and the mind, and the conscious intention is to kill the self's body and leave the mind to "enjoy" the triumph/peace/escape or whatever is the imagined outcome of the suicidal act. Suicide seen in this way is a form of acting out. The term acting out describes how we carry out a particular action or set of actions in order to bypass something, some emotional experience or conflictual state which is too difficult to face consciously. Like adolescents who steal or become promiscuous because really they are trying to make a claim on the world for something they need but feel they cannot face this neediness and/or fear they will be rejected for it. Acting out is often a substitute for remembering or facing an earlier trauma or loss or even simply something that is emotionally out of reach or too frightening to face. Its aim is to reverse or prevent recognition of the early trauma and to relieve tension. Which it might well do in the short term—but alas only temporarily; the feelings reappear so the acting out needs to be repeated.

With suicide the acting out is final—or is it? The horrible, sinister aspect of suicide is that there also remains a peculiar delusional aspect to it, namely that killing the body is indeed the conscious and often much-expressed aim, but the suicidal act is also a means to the survival of a part of the self *that wants and needs to survive*. But, and here is the rub, this surviving part is dependent on the destruction of the body and the delusion is that the mind/self will live on. Behind the suicidal act are a suicidal fantasy and a delusional conviction that part of the self will survive in order to experience the solution. This is I think the saddest and most pitiful aspect of any analysis of suicide. That the person while saying she really wants to die is actually saying at the same time that she wants to live, but that she wants to live a different life. The world of the suicide is riddled with riddles, with vague clues and hints sometimes so obscure and opaque that they could not possibly be picked up on by even the most perspicacious amongst us.

This is the unconscious trying to/not trying to be seen and heard— like a perverse game of hide and seek. The tragedy is that the individual by this point has lost touch, almost completely, with that aspect of themselves and all too often has caused the rest of us to lose sight of this too. I am not sure how many of you reading this have been closely involved with anyone who is suicidal but it is very draining, sometimes to the point at which one is tempted to wish "A plague on all your houses"! As well as this being an understandable human reaction in someone at the end of his tether, it is also a response to the aggressive wishes so unacceptable and suppressed in the suicidal person, namely to get rid of them.

Just to illustrate this aspect of the split-off nature of the suicidal act consider this: a patient reported that he had taken 199 aspirins. One had fallen on the floor and he refused to swallow it, to include it in his overdose, because it might have germs on it (Campbell & Hale, 1991, p. 288). Similarly, another person refused a doughnut four hours before a suicide attempt because he did not want to put on weight. Finally, the suffragette Emily Davidson who threw herself under the king's horse was found with a return train ticket in her pocket. Does this point to her death having been an accident, that she had no intention to kill herself, or is this another example of suicidal ambivalence?

With this in mind it is also worth a detour into the idea of accidental suicide or subintentional suicide. On examination it seems clear that many so-called accidents are not in fact entirely accidents in the sense of being entirely related to chance or the action of another. A sizeable percentage of deaths have this sub-intentional suicidal quality. Many years ago Shneidman undertook an interesting data analysis on a random sample of coroner's verdicts of deaths in Marin County, California, over a period of two years. Of these deaths, 131 were clearly categorised as suicide by the coroner, but of the remaining 843 cases 16 per cent were rated as having some participatory element to them which led to the death. In other words one sixth of all the deaths over this period in that county had some aspect of sub-intentional suicidality to them. Extrapolating this to the whole country, or indeed globally, puts suicidality in a whole new realm in terms of numbers. But to my mind it also illustrates quite dramatically the pull we have towards death and also our ambivalent relationship to the struggles of life. We smoke, we drink, we take drugs—legal and prescribed—we drive, we fight, we go to war, we have unprotected sex, we martyr ourselves to a cause, we use bad judgement about whom to be involved with, we disregard our health, and so on. In many ways these are all examples of sub-intentional suicidality—though not necessarily brought to completion. These are illustrations of the many ways in which we demonstrate our ambivalence and our anger about having a life at all! As Phillips so enigmatically puts it: "Everything depends on what we would rather do than change."

Perhaps we are all to a certain extent angry that we have to change, to grow up and face the vicissitudes of life. We seem to be able to find all sorts of ways of truncating our lives and also of narrowing its focus, of making it more unhappy and difficult than it needs to be—of having a narrow, bitter, reduced relation to it. Depression itself is an example of this, I think, as are other "illnesses" of the mind and body—a feeling of flatness, like a living death, a refusal to take part in life. And how difficult it seems for us to remain self-motivated and positive. You just have to look at the vast numbers of self-help books crowding the shelves of high street bookshops and internet links to see that this bounty might well illustrate a case of "the bigger the front the bigger the back"! If life was that easy to live "positively" we'd all be at it. Or to put in another way, maybe we need to take seriously our draw towards death in order that we have a more healthy respect for it. This takes us once again to the Freudian concept of the life and death drives, and to Kleinian ideas of love and hate—both of which are active in our relation to the world.

Life goes on because these processes work together—they are contrasting but not adversarial. In those of us who consider ourselves well-adjusted, Eros (life) and Thanatos (death) function within us in a complementary manner right across our personal and interpersonal lives. We seek out new experiences, reach out to others, and expend energy in pursuit of stimulations and satisfactions. Eros smiles over ventures such as these. There are times, though, when we need to act aggressively on the world, to protect ourselves and our interests, or to withdraw from overstimulation and exertion and seek quietude. Thanatos presides over these aggressive and risky ventures and also over restorative retirement into "downtime".

Most aspects of ordinary living, for example sex, work, and play, include both care and aggression, love and hate. So to return to the suicidal person the negotiation between these two processes has very seriously derailed. It would be a real mistake to respond only to the pill-taking patient above in terms of his wish to live, demonstrated by his rejection of the one germ-laden pill, and to ignore the aggression behind the intention to swallow all the other 199 pills! In such a person, for all sorts of complex and long-standing reasons, aggressive feelings and wishes have long been unacceptable and felt to be so dangerous that they are utterly repressed. When we view suicide only in a benign way—in a sympathetic or sorrowful way—we miss an important point about the act itself—that it is an act of aggression and of violence. If we neglect this we do a major injustice to ourselves and to the person who is suicidal.

CHAPTER SIX

The suicidal fantasy

We are now beginning to see the suicidal condition and the suicidal act are complexities that can feature and take hold in any individual. Suicide, in my view, is a standalone condition which needs its own careful analysis and understanding. It is in no particular way connected with conventional thinking about mental illness but bears better scrutiny if it is considered in and of itself. There are common aspects to suicides but it always, or nearly always, has a meaning for the individual suicide which is theirs alone. Knowing as we do that in the UK as many as seven people per day, on average, kill themselves at present recorded rates, it is important that we extend our understanding of something so deathly as suicide beyond a conventional medical view of mental illness or a socio-economic analysis of deprivation, so that we may better grasp its psychological roots and meaning and hence have more of a chance of approaching it.

Perhaps the reason why we associate suicide with illness is that it is easier for us to think of suicide in terms of pessimism and depression. If someone takes his own life then it must be because he thinks his life is not worth living. Maybe he has had an insurmountable degree of difficulty to face, a lousy start in life, unparalleled losses to deal with. All of this may well be true of certain suicides. But what these well-meaning assumptions about suffering and depression fail to appreciate, and in a way this is as the unconscious intends, is the aggression behind the act. Suicide is an act of killing and destruction. The intention at the time of the act is to both save the self and destroy the self. To kill the self's body but—and here is the deathly clincher—to keep part of the self's mind alive. As I put it at the beginning of this book, as stated by Campbell and Hale (1991), suicide is an act both for and against the self. The suicidal person is in the ultimate position of ambivalence, with life and death balanced on a knife edge. There is a wish to live and a wish to die. In the moments of suicide the hostility, rage, despair, hopelessness are all felt to be too much, but there is also a very active wish and desire to live without the pain. However, at the fatal moment of suicide the person appears to view herself almost as another person, to separate out herself from herself and hence to take out on her own body, and on the continuing lives of others, the hostility and despair that relates to past and present injuries felt to have been experienced.

In many cases of suicide the felt pain can seem recent and is often reported as such by the person herself; it seems to be related only to immediate and pressing life events—relationship breakdown, money troubles, etc. But invariably, on close examination, it has long roots going back to a perceived thwarted early life. In the suicidal individual, at the moment of suicide, it is as if the actual body is regarded as a separate being and identified with the hated stuff of life, the hated, the lost, or the never had life, and then killed off. But, and this is a crucial "but", at the same time there is a delusional belief that the self will somehow survive to benefit from the death and to have the imagined wished-for life. As Jeremy Holmes puts it: "At the suicidal moment, in order for life to be endurable, there has to be a death" (1996, p. 149).

It is important to examine this idea further because I think it goes to the core of the hidden aggression behind the act and the often missed delusory aspect which lies at the heart of most, or almost all suicides. Indeed, there may well be suicides wherein the causes seem more rational and clear, for example those of the very elderly or terminally ill, but these arguments may well be a distraction from the more complex aspects of the condition of suicide. It is far easier for most of us to understand someone taking her own life at say ninety-two years old or when in the grip of a terrible terminal illness, than to understand the death by his own hand of an apparently healthy thirty-five year old. In some ways arguments about so-called rational suicides or assisted suicide often become a way of distancing us from the main theatre of suicidality, which takes over so viciously and perniciously, in the mind of those who are in fact not ill or very old. But I want to drill down further into the deadly enactment of the suicidal mind of the person who is not terminally ill in the ordinary sense in order that we can get a much better sense of the condition. I would also argue, perhaps controversially, that there is, or there might be a deal of disguised anger in the action of an elderly person who claims they "do not want to be a burden". Perhaps such a person is also saying "Please do more" and actually railing against that which cannot be endured.

You may have noticed and you may have been surprised by my use of the word delusion. We saw in the previous chapter how suicide often contains an aspect of settling old scores, a sense of long-held grievance, of being thwarted. Often these things are buried in the unconscious— the person involved does not necessarily actively know about them. These wounds, either real or imagined, lie in deep recesses of the mind and the person will often have little or no understanding or awareness of them or of the trouble they are causing. But they take hold, they grow, they do not get worked out or resolved, and instead they fester and get mixed up and confused with real external events in later life. The person will implicate and involve others in all sorts of complicated enactments of the dramas of the mind. Colleagues will be seen as enemies and lovers as saviours. The person recreates the drama of his unhealed wounds in the people of the present and in the inevitable frustrations of the present. But invariably in this way lies disaster. Of course we all do this to some extent. We fall in love with people we see as versions of our past—our mothers, our fathers, our knowns and our unknowns. We also fall out with people who we see as versions of our past, recreating the same sort of unresolved conflicts time after time. And we also try to create ways in which old unconscious conflicts are repeated with the hope in vain that they will be laid to rest. Alas, without insight, without this being made conscious, this invariably fails. People will stubbornly refuse to take on the roles assigned and trouble invariably reappears! Or they will happily take on the punishing and exploitative aspects that suit them and keep themselves in the misery they have in some way assigned to themselves. Either way is often doomed to repetition without resolution and worse still to compounding the pain. The person may get temporary relief with a new lover or a new boss or a new house but invariably, because she has no other solution in mind, once the other parties refuse to play their parts, she recreates the same scenario once again, and so on.

In suicide something similar, but very much more deadly, is going on—behind the suicide action is a fantasy that some part of the self will survive in order to achieve the satisfaction of the act. In fact it is probably misleading to describe this as a part of the self—but because of the delusory nature of this phenomenon I think we will struggle to find words to describe it. It is more as if the person is in a bipartite state. There is the conscious wish to die with all the expressed reasons why death is the "only" option. But at the same time there is a less clearly stated, often quite unconscious, wish to survive. The suicidal person seems convinced that suicide is the right thing to do but at the same time he is also imagining life after the act—as if there is a life for him somehow separate from his death. This is what I mean by the delusional nature of the act. I am not by any means saying that suicidal people are mad, not at all. But that in order to act on this, and for it to make sense to yourself, you must have somewhere in your mind the idea that you, part of you, another you, will survive in order to think that this is a good idea in the first place! In order to believe that this action will bring you the relief or revenge or self-sacrifice that you intend it for, you are imagining yourself going on after death. In a way the suicidal person is creating his own afterlife in his mind.

In fact I am not at all sure suicide is possible without this delusional belief. The psychoanalysts Campbell and Hale, whose research included immediate interviews with people who had just survived suicide attempts and comments made by suicidal patients in psychotherapy, describe this phenomenon thus:

> The suicidal fantasy always includes a dyadic relationship between a part of the self which will survive and the body which is identified with an intolerable object. Although killing the body was indeed a conscious aim, it was, in fact a means to an end. The end was the pleasurable survival of an essential part of the self—which we will refer to as the surviving self—a self that survives in another dimension. However this survival is dependent on the destruction of the body. (1991, p. 291)

It is this that to my mind makes suicide so tragic and so seductive—the person is using a completely destructive method to try to alleviate their pain or solve life's problems, or act out their envy of others, and is also in some way believing they will survive to feel the outcome.

We can get a feel of this delusional quality and also the bipartite state of suicide when we focus on the words spoken by suicidal people and also used in suicide notes. They reveal how perspectives on death in suicidal people seem romanticised, idealised. Bizarrely they often have a life-giving rather than life-taking quality to them. The following are quotes from research undertaken by Thomas Joiner (2005), who has developed an interpersonal/psychological theory of suicidality:

> "I'll be happy when I'm dead."
> "I'll be with my mother again."
> "Everything will be OK when I'm gone."
> "It would be a beautiful death" (a patient describing a slow and graceful fall off a cliff edge).

Joiner and colleagues reflect on how these sorts of statement suggest a sense of "belonging" to death and a sense of connectedness to the concept of death, the saviour death, the escape death, the repairer or ender of emotional pain death. In this way they note death has become confused with life-sustaining qualities. In fact when you jump off a cliff edge there is very little that is graceful or slow about it—it is fast, painful, and violent and you end impaled, bloodied, broken, and dead on the rocks below. This shows how the idea (and ideal) of death is fused with notions and knowledge gained from life. Actually we know nothing of death, even those of us who are religious. The suicidal person in his split state ascribes to death things only known about through knowledge of living. In this way he creates his own afterlife based on what he wishes for, but feels denied of, in life. The suicidal person also becomes signed up to the concept of death as inevitable—when and why he comes to this deadly conclusion is as individual as it gets.

Joiner finds three factors that mark those most at risk of death: the feeling of being a burden on loved ones; the sense of isolation; and, chillingly, the learned ability to hurt oneself. Professor O'Connor from Glasgow University's suicide research centre describes the accompanying sense of entrapment, stating that suicidal people demonstrate "a high sensitivity to cues in the environment signalling defeat and a sense of entrapment" (O'Connor, Smyth, Ferguson, Ryan, & Williams, 2013, p. 1138). The writer David Foster Wallace who killed himself in

2008 wrote of suicidal people as suffering from an "invisible agony" that reaches such an unendurable level that they will kill themselves in "the same way a trapped person will eventually jump from the window of a burning high rise". The journalist Cosmo Landesman, whose son Jack killed himself in 2015 aged twenty-nine, was mystified and refreshingly honest about his son's death:

> I don't believe he died because of cuts in public funding for mental health services, or because of those much cited suicide factors such as anxiety and depression. He died because he wanted the perpetual torment of his mind to stop. He was absolutely convinced there was no alternative to suicide. What happened to his mind—my broken brain—as he called it—and what is happening to so many other men is a mystery to me. (interview in *The Sunday Times*, December 6, 2015)

In desperation Landesman disarmingly talks of offering his son £50 to go running with him every day for half an hour for just one week: "I promise you exercise will make you feel so much better." His son merely smiled and said: "Thanks, but I'd rather kill myself than go jogging." This it seems to me is a statement of some aggression and of some contempt. Is Jack making an attack on life itself and on those, like his own father, who live it and who gave it to him in the first place and who by this point was reduced to desperately trying to bribe him into it, in the face of his determined rejection of it?

It is now necessary to explore in more detail the concept of suicidal fantasy. Herein lies the deadly heart of the matter of suicide. Behind every suicide, we could say, there exists a suicidal fantasy and at the time of acting out the suicide this has distorted the person's view of reality such that it has the power of a delusional conviction. The delusion being that part, or even the whole, of the self will survive in order to experience the "gain" of the action. But this survival is dependent on the death of the body. This idea is not just essential to our understanding of suicide and to the possibility of working through suicidality but also I think to confusion around the notion of choice. For the most part we see ourselves operating throughout life having options and exercising choices. Consequently we can readily accept suicide as a person's choice without realising that choice and suicide may well be irreconcilable notions. This notion of choice fails to recognise the power of the grip of the fantasy and the delusional nature of thinking at the time of suicide.

Alvarez (1971) describes this as the "closed world of suicide", an either/ or state where there are only two options—the desired life or the necessary death. Choices and options plural at this point are just not in the mind. The suicidal person believes she has no choice but to act out the fantasy.

Hale and Campbell describe at least five main types of suicidal fantasy or theme, each of which exemplifies the dyadic relationship between the surviving self and the body that is to be killed off. In each person one type of fantasy may dominate but they are not necessarily mutually exclusive. First is the merging fantasy which can be seen to underpin all other forms of suicidal fantasy. Here the person sees death as a peaceful return to nature, a release from life's impossible demands, a regression back to an infantile, uroboric, fused state of blissful nothingness, omnipotently at one with the world. The fantasy is that in death the self will survive as in a state akin to that of a peaceful sleeping infant untroubled by the miseries and realities of adulthood. Meanwhile the body is killed off because it represents that which frustrates and disappoints this dream. It is worth noting the language of the suicidal person as this will often reveal the nature of the fantasy or fantasies—with the merging fantasy the person will talk of just wanting peace, to sleep forever, of having had enough, etc. The type of method chosen for suicide also I think underlines the nature of the fantasy. With the merging fantasy it is likely that an overdose would be the chosen method.

Second, Hale and Campbell describe the revenge fantasy which centres on the impact the suicide will actually have on others. In this case the aggression is much more conscious—many who act out this kind of vengeful fantasy leave notes for those closest to them which often contain phrases which are palpably full of hate as in:

> "I hope you're sorry now."
> "I cannot live without you. I may as well be dead."
> "Maybe now you'll see what you are missing."

Other examples more subtly hint at the hate, and project guilt onto the survivor from the grave: "Please don't think you could have done anything to help me, please don't feel guilty." (The examples are taken from Shneidman, 1996, pp. 14–15, and the author's own reportage.)

At the same time the person will often choose a more violent form of death—hanging or shooting—and horribly public or in the family home. It is unfortunately common for family members to come home to find the suicidal person hanging in the hallway or gassed in the garage. Finding the dead person and/or being in receipt of a suicide note like this is felt as a devastating attack. This is as intended. The revenge suicide has a very marked feel of sadism, with the surviving self "enjoying" the role in the afterlife as observer of the suffering of those left behind. "They" deserve it "because they did not love me enough". There is a marked sense of retaliation and triumph. This kind of suicide may often be preceded by threats of suicide to emotionally blackmail others. Thus if the suicide is carried out it will also leave the survivors with complex and confused feelings, as the guilt they feel may cause them to deny the anger and relief which the suicide may also bring them but to which it is impossible to admit. It takes a huge amount of courage to face up to this kind of dynamic.

A third fantasy is almost the reverse of the revenge fantasy, that of self-punishment. Here the enactment is rooted in guilt and self-blame and the overarching feeling is one of masochism as opposed to sadism— the world is crap and it is all my fault. This fantasy is full of terms of self-abasement, self-loathing, and low self-worth. But beneath this lurks also a hostility to the world for being so troublesome and for causing so much pain, misery, and suffering and perhaps for feeding a false story about how perfect life should be. Adolescents often feel very guilty and self-punishing about their feelings, about their bodies, about their thoughts, and most notably about their imperfections and limits. They also have very little experience of negotiating their way through this terrain. With rising expectations in this country around academic success, and having had very little experience of failure, academic but perfectionist young men and women are particularly susceptible to this kind of delusional thinking. They believe they have to be perfect and they do not know how to accept the limits and frustrations when they discover they are not. They believe they must be better than they are and that the world will not love them or tolerate them if they are not. One deeply troubled student at one of the UK's leading academic universities, on receiving a mark of 100 per cent in a mid-term exam, said that "It was not the right sort of 100 per cent." He was not able to be satisfied even with this.

With the next form of fantasy—what Hale and Campbell call an elimination fantasy—here the actual body is experienced as something mad or bad and has to be destroyed for the self to survive. The surviving self kills off the killer body—this is in a twisted way a kind of action of self-reservation! Kill the body because it is seen to be turning against the self with its bad looks and bad thoughts which cannot be negotiated. Often suicide of this type will involve cutting or slashing the body or blowing away the bad mind/brains. Once again young people are particularly susceptible to this kind of thinking. The adolescent body throws up all sorts of physical changes which can be experienced as unacceptable, particularly when linked to sexual thoughts and feelings which are felt to be unsafe, unwanted, or bewildering. Beneath the elimination fantasy lies the merging fantasy—a wish to get away from the smelly, hairy, oozing, spotty, urgent, raging body of puberty to the idealised state of smooth-bodied, cherubic infancy. Chad Varah, the founder of the Samaritans, is reputed to have started the work after officiating at the funeral of a fourteen-year-old girl who killed herself after being mortified and shamed as a result of her first menstruation.

Finally Hale and Campbell describe the dicing with death fantasy or deadly risk taking. This can take obvious forms such as drink-driving, drug taking, extreme risk taking in sport etc. These activities and behaviours in and of themselves may not necessarily lead to death, and risk takers per se do not exceed the limits of their bodies or the world, but the proposal is that the person is both trying to attract and attack the care of the Other. By taking really extreme risks the person is saying, "Look at me, rescue me. I'm not responsible for what happens to me but you—fantasised mother I never had—you make me safe or else!" This has a strong sadomasochistic flavour to it.

To these five themes I would also add that of the hero or anti-hero fantasy where the person identifies with another or an idea of heroism/ perfection and imagines his death will allow him to live on in the identification with the hero. Thus celebrity suicides, such as that of Kurt Cobain in 1994, which occur for all sorts of individual intrapsychic reasons, private and deeply personal to that individual, can trigger clusters of "copycat" suicides. Young people are once again particularly susceptible to this kind of influence. Rock stars, film stars who appear to have lived on the edge and died young, attract a particular kind of attention and identification which leads to vulnerable and susceptible young people thinking they will be thought of, and remembered, as being just like, for example, Kurt Cobain or Amy Winehouse. "If I die like them then I am like them." Through their death such young people will fantasise that they will gain the sort of glory and attention they feel is so lacking in their ordinary lives, or, worse, their abused, vandalised, or alienated real lives. It is hard to feel you are enough of a self to withstand the ordinary injuries of life, let alone the truly serious traumas that do befall some youngsters.

This sort of copycat suicide/hero identification is a well-known phenomenon, described in scores of academic studies. It is sometimes known as the Werther effect, after Goethe's novel of 1774, *The Sorrows of Young Werther*, in which a young artist shoots himself after an ill-fated love affair. The publication of the novel seemed to trigger a series of suicides across Europe by the same method attributed to the hero of the novel. This led to the text being banned in some countries. It would seem that in cases such as these the individual, often a young person, is influenced by the idea of fame or even notoriety, perhaps because of an unmet or low sense of self and identity. The idea of fame by death "appeals". "I am a nobody in life but I can be a somebody in death."

Current research shows that copycat victims do not always follow on from famous deaths. They also occur among groups which come from similar backgrounds. Individuals in these cases are at greatest risk if they know other victims. The series of tragic suicides in Bridgend in South Wales between 2007 and 2008 would appear to support this view. Seventeen young people between the ages of fifteen and twenty-seven killed themselves, all of them bar one by hanging. They did not know each other that well but were, broadly speaking, of the same demographic and similar age group. They comprised both young men and young women. Suicide clusters like these are not in fact uncommon and with social networking such clusters can be from a much wider geographical range than ever before.

There is also a potential link here to terrorist suicide—the dangerous seduction of an ideology that persuades you that you will become a hero, a someone, a holy martyr for a cause bigger than you, and not a nobody. The fury against the world for the personal, political, or religious injustice you have experienced is enacted by the killing of both self and others. Perhaps the suicidal terrorist has the motivation of the revenge and hero fantasy underlying such actions.

I have gone into some detail in outlining these various forms of suicidal fantasy in order to emphasise what an important working concept this is in understanding how to work with a suicidal person and how to help make conscious his aggression and the fantasy behind his suicidal intentions. The ability to be able to think with the person about his suicidality is crucial. These ideas also help those of us involved in treating or working with those who are suicidal to be able to pick up indirect clues, to confront these, to think, to work hard, to gain ground, and to not be terrified away from it all. I am also absorbed by this notion of suicidal fantasy and delusional conviction because I have experienced it many times first hand—when talking to suicidal people in my clinical work—but primarily in coming to understand my sister's suicide. I will give some details of this because her suicide exemplified the revenge fantasy quite chillingly.

At the time of Olivia's suicide I was twenty-six and she was twenty-seven. In her pre-suicidal state(s) she was sometimes in hospital, sometimes in her own flat in a halfway house, but often staying with me and my flatmates. I was greatly supported by them at the time. After her death one of my other sisters and I had to clear out her room. As you can imagine this was dreadfully harrowing and we did it as best we could. In the process we gave my flatmates a bag full of Olivia's writings and jottings to put somewhere safe until I could face going through them. I didn't feel able to do this until some three years or so later and what I found was quite extensive—Olivia had always kept long and detailed diaries, written poetry, musings, as well as transcribed poems that resonated with her. Her output appeared to increase as she became more depressed and more suicidal. It all proved difficult reading but it was also slightly irritating, very morbid, and rather one-dimensional, and as I continued to read I remember feeling awash with grief and sadness but also increasingly angry—probably for the first time since her death and maybe for the first time in my life. Going through it I found the following extract which I believe, from the dates, was written about three months before she killed herself. It is the barest outline of a very bad novel which is a terribly thinly disguised account of our family. I saw it then and see it now as a revelation of the rage, hatred, and envy she felt towards us all. How conscious she was of this I am not sure but it belies what she had always felt at some level throughout her short life. In the outline she details how the novel will portray each of the five Ryan children (for Ryan read Murphy, our family name) and their respective falls from grace following the death by suicide of the central character Cressida at twenty-seven. Here it is just as I found it in her notebook:

Benedict—eldest and only son—travel and alcohol, eventually destroyed by both and dies in Africa of liver disease.

Hermione—marries and grows away from family, has two children but marriage breaks up. Absolute hatred for mother, disappears virtually and is bitter for rest of her life.

Cressida—commits suicide at 26/27.

Nerissa—drops out entirely after Cressida's death, cannot cope—becomes a junkie. Hatred of men.

Miranda—lack of application or direction in life, ends up getting involved in Irish republican movement, jailed or killed.

Even now as I write this I feel the same mixture of feelings as I did the very first time I read this—moved, embarrassed, and bloody furious with her—how dare she depict us/me like that! But I see it also as an absolute humdinger of an example of the revenge fantasy writ large. If she was going she was going to take us all down with her. All of us in this story are targets of her vengeance and of her envious destructiveness. Within this terrible tale is contained the hate she felt towards those who could not give her what she needed and the envy she felt towards the rest of us for supposedly having what she did not. This small lamentable extract showed me more than any theory could have done how she felt—she had to go and she was going to sink us with her, for her lack and her rage and her envy were unbearable. Because it is unbearable it requires an extreme imagination and in the end an extreme solution. The destructive nature of her suicide was and is devastating for all of us in the family who remained. In a family, whatever the shape it takes, a suicide is an act of destruction for the family as well as of the individual who dies, and it is also an expression of the family's difficulties in all its complexity. Those difficulties do not go away when the suicide victim dies. The family is left to survive as best it can, and often its members are not able to do so. The risks of death by suicide to survivors of suicide is far higher than those untouched by it. Suicide is about relationship, it is an interpersonal act. It is a communication too. Olivia's notebooks told me a whole load of stuff I sort of knew but didn't want to know and about which I was, at the time, completely out of my depth. I wish upon wish that we could have got to our mutual hatred and envy as sisters earlier, more easily and more safely. Instead, because of the various challenges in the family, we were forced to stay tightly bound together—she and I clung to each other as we grew up as if our lives depended on it; as if we were adrift on some very scary seas in a badly made hand-crafted life raft. It didn't really keep the water out that well.

The tragedy of suicide as an act of destruction is that, for Olivia and for so many others who kill themselves, the aggression remains largely unconscious and unknown by others. We see aspects of depression, psychological damage, pain, messed up lives, etc., and we try to treat these and help, but we all too often don't get hold of the aggression until it is too late. Suicide picks away at its victims in such a way as to exclude others and their attentions. That's part of its anatomy. The closed world of suicide. Wishing you could have done more, feeling guilty, feeling you should have been more attentive—all of that is so very understandable after a suicide but it is missing the point. The suicidal person wasn't thinking of you at the time. We aren't there when the loved one kills herself because she deliberately and calculatingly doesn't want us to be there. She picks the time, the method, the place precisely with our absence and, in the case of revenge, our devastation in mind.

Olivia died on her own. She meant to get away with it—her suicide was certainly no accidental overdose—it was well researched and carried out properly. She went away and we were left forever in the wrong and wronged, like the damned who can never make amends.

CHAPTER SEVEN

Working through

In the previous chapter I explained that suicide, as I have come to see it, is largely a standalone condition. That is to say that while in some ways suicide may be connected to aspects of what we commonly think of as illness, it remains primarily, in and of itself, a drama of the mind; a peculiar condition into which the mind twists itself. The soil for suicidality is usually deep and the causes are often unclear and unknown to the person involved, having a largely unconscious aspect. And one of the most important unconscious elements in play in any act of suicide is aggression or the acting out of hate.

Consequently suicidality is often hard to spot, hard to fathom, and hard to treat. Combine these factors with its notorious qualities of dissembling, impulsiveness, and lethality, and it is not surprising that so many people are able to successfully kill themselves. Sadly those who do take their own lives are not confined to the untreated—a high proportion of those in the UK who do take their own lives are, at the time of their death, in some sort of mental health treatment or in the care of a general practice or mental health team. And while we can argue about what might be the right or wrong treatment for those who are suicidal it might be more helpful to come at ideas about treatment in a way that is geared towards the individual state of mind. There are a great many health professionals—doctors, psychologists, psychotherapists, and counsellors who could be well placed to work with the suicidal in ways that will have a greater impact than is currently realised if they are enabled to contain and think about suicide with the person at risk. All too often clinicians are trained and instructed to assess suicidality by means of questionnaires or inventories but then left floundering with very inadequate resources and support when a suicide is identified. When it comes to suicide it is the better part of valour and of helpfulness to move beyond debates about treatment models and instead to fully take on what this suicide means for this person, and to work through the suicidality of the person *with that person as an individual*.

As we have already noted suicide prediction is notoriously difficult. As Shneidman says: "Most people who commit suicide talk about it; most people who talk about suicide do not commit it. Which to believe?" (1996, p. 57). This is an important statement about the strange and difficult conundrum of suicide and in particular of suicide risk assessment. It highlights how difficult is the whole territory of identifying and predicting suicide risk in any individual.

Certainly there has been a growth of very useful research into suicide risk in recent years which has largely thrown better light on, and more statistical data about, the factors which might increase suicide risk and also point to suicidality. Risk assessment tools, questionnaires, and inventories based on this research are now commonly used by medical, psychotherapy, and psychological practitioners and are now required, as part of generic assessment processes, in the NHS and other organisations. There are many different versions in use today. The intention of such instruments is to guide the practitioner through the process of identifying so-called risk factors in the patient. They all in essence cover the same sort of ground: social and occupational factors; age; demography; psychopathology; mental and physical health; previous self-injury/suicide attempts; alcohol or substance abuse; family history and make-up (including history of sexual or physical abuse); significant traumatic events; relational factors; sexuality; etc. Andrew Reeves in his study *Counselling Suicidal Clients* provides a very useful overview of such risk factors in relation to current research (2010, pp. 34–38). Such tools and inventories in use in the UK today vary in their sophistication and depth and range from, for example, the Suicide Status Form developed as part of the CAMS (Collaborative Assessment and Management of Suicide) (Jobes, 2006) to the more commonly used such as the Beck

Scale for Suicide Ideation (BSS) (Beck, 1991), and the Reasons for Living Inventory (RFL) (Linehan, Goodstein, Nielsen, & Chiles, 1983), which generally receive positive reviews. The BSS is an interviewer administered tool that purports to measure imminent threat of suicide. The RFL is a self-report instrument that focuses on the person's reasons for not killing himself (or herself). The Modified Scale for Suicide Ideation (MSSI) (Miller, Norman, Bishop, & Dow, 1986) establishes the intensity of suicidal ideas by addressing the desire for suicide, preparation, and the patient's capability to make the attempt. The Suicide Intent Scale (Beck, Resnick, & Lettieri, 1974) evaluates the suicidal intent of individuals who have survived a suicide attempt, to help in the prediction of whether they will to go on to complete a suicide (Cole-King, Parker, Williams, & Platt, 2013, pp. 284–291).

The thinking behind research linking risk factors to prediction in this way might at first glance seem relatively straightforward—undertake research to identify risk factors; design and test tools that will identify high suicide (and other risk) factors in an individual; establish his risk and give the correct treatment. Certainly for practitioners, assessment has always been an essential starting point in identifying what the matter might be and whether a particular approach or treatment will be of benefit. To this end any overall psychological assessment of a patient has always needed to include assessment of certain risk factors and these days might well include the use of a tool. But unfortunately suicide risk assessment, and indeed overall psychological assessment, is a much more complex intervention than just completing a form, the results of which can often be misleading. It is not by any means a totally predictable process and is influenced by the practitioner, by the patient's sense of or lack of trust, and/or determination to withhold, and/or dissociation, and of course by organisational factors. Do you tell the truth about your suicidal thoughts if you fear you will be deemed mentally ill? Do you tell the truth about your suicidality when it might feel vital to you to keep it up your sleeve as a protective or unconscious act of aggression? Irrespective of competence and experience, attempting to predict whether a patient will attempt to end his life is *de facto* difficult and unclear, *not* simple and predictable as the risk assessment advocates would have us believe. Stigma and fear around suicide can prevent clinicians from really asking patients about their suicidal thoughts. Patients are also deterred from disclosing suicidal thoughts because they may feel unsafe and compromised. Suicide is also a massively ambivalent and contrary state of mind as we have seen, with all sort of unconscious and aggressive intentions underlying it. Inevitably this leads to inconsistencies and omissions, deliberate or otherwise, in both reporting and in hearing and properly understanding suicidal thoughts. For example, a particular patient may well speak of suicidal thoughts to a friend or relative or GP but not disclose them to another specialist clinician or indeed *vice versa*. A suicidal person may tell someone who is on the other side of the world that she has just taken an overdose but not tell her flatmate who is asleep in the next room.

We need to be aware that suicidality is a dynamic relational process with largely unconscious aspects, with suicidal thoughts changing over time for reasons that are not easy to fathom by the person having them, let alone the well intentioned clinician. Suicidality is not something that conventional tick box risk assessment tools can easily or accurately manifest. In fact suicide is an event with a low base rate, meaning the odds are low that we can predict that a member of a specified population group (e.g., men) will have a certain characteristic, suicidality, assuming that we know nothing else about this person other than that he is a member of the population we are examining. This makes it extremely difficult to devise measures with adequate positive value to predict suicide. In summary, research has generated almost exclusively *general* correlations but fails to say much about how we can recognise the risk of suicide in an individual and, more important, where they are on their path to actually acting on this, let alone their private, personal narrative and unconscious fantasy that sustains their suicidality. As Andrew Reeves states:

> The factor based understanding of suicidality has undoubtedly informed approaches to risk assessment. Many existing risk assessment tools and questionnaires are based around the identification and subsequent weighting of such factors by the assessing counsellor. Their efficacy in identifying suicide risk and in helping to increase rates of suicide prediction in general terms could be asserted; the same degree of efficacy with individuals is less clear. (2010, p. 33)

In other words we may well have got much better at predicting a whole range of high-risk groups and factors but this does not amount to much when it comes to the individual, and, more important, when it comes to working with and treating an individual who is suicidal.

More important still, in terms of ongoing treatment, it can be seriously misleading to clinicians and patients alike to imply that using risk assessment tools alone will predict suicidality and will then lead to effective treatment outcomes (Bolton, Gunnell, & Turecki, 2015, h4978). This can lead to a worrying fear that getting it right or wrong is the fault of the clinician, leading to overprotective or defensive practice which is not always in the interests of the patient. What might be more helpful is for clinicians to have in mind in any initial interview that consideration of suicidal thoughts and behaviour is an important intention. The best approach to ascertaining whether there is any suicidal ideation on first meeting a patient is to ask! And this is best achieved by way of a sensitive, dialogic, relational, professional, fearless, and well informed clinical encounter, whereby the practitioner diligently identifies all aspects of the person's state of mind and history to date by asking him to talk about himself and then listens to what he says, how he says it, and also listens to what he omits. This will include specific questions about suicide, and also identify protective factors, in order to ascertain his state of mind but also his disposition to his life. Once this is known to some extent the process of establishing an approach that might help him can be elaborated together with him.

With greater emphasis on a research and risk assessment paradigm only we may fail to hear the patient's own thoughts and feelings, and miss hearing about her individual pain and story. We may miss hearing how feeling suicidal may also act as a protective factor. In the hands of an inexperienced worker or in an organisation that predetermines treatment on the basis of risk factors, this, in and of itself, may reinforce the experience the person has had in the world, about the world, and her relationship to it. It is often very early misattunement and abandonment (abandonment which is often repeated when the patient once identified as suicidal is referred on to another clinician or service) which has contributed to her suicidality. Risk assessment forms are often used in GP surgeries, IAPT services, mental health teams, etc. to triage the person out of the service—"You are suicidal, your risk factors show this, you are too risky for this service, so we are referring you on." I am not arguing against using questionnaires or inventories in order to discover more about a person who is seeking help but this absolutely must be attached to a thoughtful, thorough, confident, experienced, and relational approach and must bear in mind the individual. Simply put, not everyone is able to answer questions on a questionnaire and the answers given can very often be misleading and dissembling—features of the ambivalence and dissociative qualities of the suicidal state of mind.

Dr Alys Cole-King and colleagues (Cole-King, Green, Gask, Hines, & Platt, 2013, pp. 276–283) have developed a method of assessing suicidality based on a compassionate and active approach to suicide prevention. Their training programme Connecting with People, in which they promote the establishment of a therapeutic alliance and safe relationship between clinician and patient, is matched with a comprehensive risk assessment. This emphasis on compassion, containment, and relationship will comes as no surprise to counsellors and psychotherapists for whom the establishment of a therapeutic alliance is fundamental to working with any patient. However, it is gratifying, albeit confounding that this is still resisted in some medical circles, to note that the Connecting with People approach now forms part of the Royal College of Psychiatry education programme.

Andrew Reeves discusses his own experience of patients who, having had various psychiatric and medical treatments and interventions, speak of having never had the opportunity of talking about their difficulties in this relational, individual way. He quotes a client thus: "I've never really talked about this, you know. I've been in and out of hospital countless times but have never really been asked about how I feel." (2010, p. 11). Relational clinical work, such as that done within psychotherapy and counselling, is really a very good option for the successful treatment of suicidal people, but it is also a difficult and complex option for both patient and clinician, requiring high levels of clinical competency, confidence, professionalism, theoretical understanding, and above all containment. Here we are talking about hard, long-term, complex, painful, very disturbing, worrying, and highly finessed work. Like Reeves I do think counsellors, psychotherapists, and analysts can be ideally placed to work with a large proportion of those with suicidal ideation and intention because, regardless of their theoretical approach, the treatment approach is designed specifically to focus on the narrative and the unconscious world of the individual patient for its own sake, and not within the context of a medical diagnosis or within any particular social, health, economic, legal, organisational, or other agenda.

In general, medical practice emphasises disease, diagnosis, and treatment, and often the suicidal person will not fit neatly into these categories or even present within a medical context. By contrast the general aim of the psychotherapeutic endeavour, in particular the psychoanalytic endeavour, is to encourage free association, to allow the unconscious to be made conscious, to say as openly as possible whatever is in the mind without fear of judgement. To emphatically *not* take things at face value that others in other contexts might so take. And this is, by and large, a crucial and very apposite endeavour for those who are suicidal because it allows that which is out of reach, out of discourse, felt to be too appalling or unacceptable to be acknowledged, to be thought about. It allows our ambivalence about life and death, love and hate to be known and, importantly, to be survived with and by another. It allows someone who is suicidal to articulate their suicidal wishes and to find important meaning in them—to uncover what their suicidal fantasy is an expression of and about—and ultimately, if possible, to use these insights to move beyond suicide. In other words to find out about themselves, to face up to themselves, to face up to their fury and disappointment with the world, to face up to the things and people they have lost, the things and people theywill never have, the fact that they don't have to be anything in particular to live—to accept they are just as sad, messed up, hard done by, incomplete, imperfect, ashamed, and insecure as the rest of us.

Many people find knowing what their feelings are, and thinking about them, very problematic. Consequently feelings are got rid of by actions, by drugs, by eating, by sex, by all sorts of things ... But the capacity to be able to feel and to contain and manage one's feelings is essential for a healthy mental life. The development of the ability to self-reflect on one's own and others' feelings comes very early in our development and is helped by the presence of good enough adult care that can provide the beginnings of this framework in the child. This helps establish good boundaries around and about the self. "This is me, that is you." Peter Fonagy's work on thinking and mentalizing—the ability to represent mental events—is helpful here. He stresses: "The capacity to conceive of the contents of one's own, as well as the object's mind, is an important requisite for normal (object) relationships" (1991, p. 649). I would add that the capacity to contain or bear what is being felt is also crucial for normal relationships and normal survival in the world. Therapeutic work with someone who does not know or cannot bear their feelings and thoughts is so important because it makes possible, among many other aspects, two important things which are particularly crucial for the suicidal person:

- A safe place for the person to discover what their feelings actually are
- A relationship between the person and another person (the therapist) in which these feelings can be thought about, understood, and not got rid of because they are regarded as too terrible, terrifying, or impossible.

If this was not important enough there is something even more crucial to the project of psychotherapy that is arguably vital, but very confounding, which enables the proper working through of suicidality; namely *trust*. Trust that what the patient says to her psychotherapist is entirely confidential, is in fact privileged. Here in the UK registered counsellors, psychotherapists, psychoanalysts, and psychologists are bound by professional codes of practice and ethics. This is helpful but in a way only up to a point. Some of these codes imply that the therapist has to maintain a balance between the patient's right to confidentiality, with the nod to autonomy and self-determination, and the patient's safety. This can be very unclear for the therapist and it is quite difficult, if not impossible, to see where these two aspects deviate from each other. In the UK it is not a legal requirement to report concerns about suicide. However, therapists employed by organisations to deliver a therapeutic service may be subject to disclosure requirements by the organisation. Consequently this territory can get very muddled and often therapists fear they will be in breach of either legal or ethical parameters if they do not disclose suicidal risk. The notion of whether the patient has capacity under the Mental Capacity Act 2005 can further muddy these waters. In fact patients have a right under law, not just under professional codes, to expect that a therapeutic relationship remains confidential. This includes those patients who talk about suicidal thoughts and feelings. But suicide is often mistakenly taken to be contiguous with mental illness—that anyone who is expressing suicidal thoughts must be suffering from a mental illness. But as we have seen this is not the case. True, those with a diagnosed form of mental illness are considered to be at higher risk of suicide within the parameters of risk assessment, but it is incorrect to assume that anyone expressing suicidal thoughts is mentally ill and therefore may not have capacity under the Act. This way leads to disaster for the therapeutic endeavour if the clinician, with good intent, feels they must always disclose any or every patient's suicidal thoughts and feelings. As Reeves puts it, "If the counsellor believes that their adult client retains mental capacity, despite being profoundly distressed and suicidal (using the criteria specified for capacity under the Act and detailed in the chapter) they do not have an automatic right to break confidentiality in the absence of client consent, and would potentially be acting in breach of their contract with the client." (2010, p. 66). But of course, as Reeves goes onto discuss, there are important and helpful ways in which, within the therapeutic relationship, the clinician can encourage a patient at great risk to consult with their GP, psychiatrist, CMHT, crisis team, etc., and in so doing may gain the patient's consent to consult with these colleagues directly.

It is terribly important that clinicians understand the legal and ethical parameters surrounding this work. For me the most important point to make is that what lies at the heart of psychotherapy, unlike in any other arena, is the possibility of disclosure of what is in the mind that cannot be tolerated. This is what makes psychotherapy the near-perfect treatment for suicidality. The American born British psychoanalyst Christopher Bollas, together with lawyer David Sandelson, explore this fascinating territory in their book *The New Informants* (1995) in which they describe what they see as a betrayal of, and intrusion into, the privilege of confidentiality by way of the increasing recording requirements, legal demands for testimony, care pathway plans, etc. currently being imposed on therapists. In contrast to the prevailing wind of disclosure and risk aversion at all costs, the authors make the case for absolute confidentiality if psychotherapy is to be effective:

> The right to say what is on one's mind in psychotherapy is not restricted—as it is in legal or medical consultations—to the expression of conscious ideas. At the heart of the free associative process is a method for the unpremeditated disclosure of whatever crosses the patient's mind. In order to do this, *he must trust that the clinician will not take him at his word*, but will instead regard the expression of thought as the means to liberate unconscious ideas, memories, and feelings that contribute to his mental suffering and disturbed relations. (pp. 60–61; italics added)

If a patient feels that by his disclosing suicidal thoughts, murderous destructive feelings, or unacceptable behaviours, the therapist will break confidentiality and report these disclosures, then he will keep these to himself or at least self-censor. In fact, often the patient might try to set up the therapist, test the therapist's ability to contain these unbearable feelings—all of which is grist to the mill of working through. For sure the suicidal patient puts the therapist between a rock and a hard place (the place he feels himself to be in), but this is all part and parcel of working through. If instead the therapist acted only on the patient's disclosure of the wish to kill himself, and sent him immediately to a mental health team or psychiatrist or hospital, she would be missing the other important part of the work, namely the patient's wish to live and the patient's fantasy that someone else can/should be responsible for his self-destructive actions towards his body. And, most important, what might be missed is the ambivalence at the heart of suicide. Certainly any attempts at a sort of therapeutic blackmail need to be taken seriously by the clinician—sometimes the patient does actually know she is not safe in her own hands—but this needs to be understood and managed within the ongoing analytic work through an interpretation of the fear that the therapist is abandoning the patient together, with exploration as to how the patient might personally respond to her own lack of safety, for example by attending GP or psychiatric appointments during the therapist's holiday, between sessions, taking appropriate medication, staying with safe people, phoning Samaritans. In fact it is difficult, if not impossible, for a therapist working with this degree of suicidality not to be placed at some point in a double bind—this is the nature of this particular beast. The therapist needs to know what she can do and what she cannot do. This a serious point because it is the therapist's ability to contain, interpret, judge, and respond to the suicidal blackmail, and how they do this, that makes the work possible. The suicidal patient may at this point in part be using the suicidality to control and regulate the relationship, and fears about relationship in general.

At these crisis/critical points more contact might be preferable, typically more than once per week. Phone calls may also be useful. But the therapist needs also to be careful—too much contact can lead to overdependence and a reinforcement that the patient is not to be trusted with herself and that the therapy/therapist is not able to survive her attacks. It may also undermine efforts to help the person learn to cope and manage using her own self-soothing techniques. However, too little contact, or a disregard for the patient's need for more help at this time, may miss the terror the patient feels that they are not safe in their own hands and can reinforce a sense of isolation and abandonment, again reinforcing the original thwart. The decision needs to be talked about, explored together, and all aspects considered jointly to find the right balance. This is very hard work but essential if the therapist is about to take a break for example. However, it is also essential that the therapist takes normal holiday breaks so that she does not get burnt out by the patient, but also so that the suicidal patient's wish to be treated in a special way, to be special, is acknowledged but not submitted to.

The therapist can interpret this: can suggest that the patient has the idea of suicide, because of fears of abandonment, annihilation, and rejection. The idea is to be able to manage the difficult things about therapy/relationship/life without resorting to suicide. So in the first place this is how the therapy is conducted—without threats. You enable the patient to see that therapy can only continue if the patient remains alive and you then interpret their attacks on themselves as attacks on the therapy and vice versa. This is not the same as making a suicide contract. Personally I do not recommend the use of promises or contracts extracted from patients not to kill themselves while in therapy. In a way these sorts of deals are not necessary if the important interpretations about attacks on the therapy are made, and secondly they may reinforce an original distrustful relational dynamic wherein the person was always told what not to do. They will also potentially silence the patient in talking about their suicidality, the very thing that needs to be talked about and known about, in particular the nature of the unconscious fantasy. Dr Eoin Galavan, clinical lead for the North Dublin Suicide Assessment and Treatment Service, which utilises the CAMS model based on David Jobes's collaborative model (2006), also eschews the use of "safety contracts". He states, of suicide contracts:

> They are neither contracts nor do they ensure safety. Instead they can become a coercive extraction of a promise to not do things when feeling suicidal. … The alternative is to develop a treatment plan that includes references to what the patient will do if they feel suicidal. This involves a good faith commitment by both parties to earnestly engage in a plan of active clinical work for a mutually agreed period of time. (2014, p. 53)

The CAMS approach is a lot more structured than many therapists may favour but at the heart of this model lie the same important aspects of containment, boundaries, and non-collusion essential to therapeutic working through for the suicidal individual.

To return to the general analytic method, this is intended to facilitate the arrival, albeit fraught and difficult, at psychic truth. As Bollas succinctly puts it: "The analyst is not in his mind at least failing to take the patient's life seriously. Indeed, it is his view that only by restraining the kind of response available to the patient from everyone else in life—it is after all easy enough for anyone to get advice from a friend or a different kind of professional—means that he can be true to the patient's psychic reality" (Bollas & Sandelson, 1995, p. 63). In the case of suicide there are plenty of professionals available to offer medication, psychiatric help, crisis plans, telephone support, inpatient admission (although these days this is increasingly rare), as necessary, but there are none other than the psychotherapeutic clinician who will be able to explore the meaning of the suicidal fantasy and the unconscious aggression behind it while helping the patient to contain the unbearableness of the feelings themselves. There are all manner of really useful and helpful interventions—medical, palliative, behavioural, etc. And none of these need be mutually exclusive from therapy. However, I am emphasising the importance, the uniqueness of the psychotherapeutic alliance because it offers a combination of containment and absolute confidentiality which enables the fullest exploration of the unconscious and an exploration of suicidality wherein the intolerable and sometimes daily intense feelings of hopelessness, desperation, and isolation can be acknowledged and borne and at the same time the elements of hidden and repressed aggression can be made known.

As Shneidman puts it, if, in the therapy, you can address "the individual's perturbation (the sense of things being wrong) *and what this may be about*, that person's lethality (the pressure to get out of it by suicide) will decrease as the perturbation is reduced" (1996, p. 8). But we also need to remember that the person will not necessarily consciously know what is wrong, or at least all of what is wrong—the road to finding out can be a very long road in therapeutic terms—so in times of suicidal crisis anything else that helps through the crisis is of paramount importance—medications, crisis team, Samaritans, a good supportive GP, CPN, psychiatrist, etc., as long as the people involved know what they are doing and are not frightened by the person's suicidality. In therapeutic work with suicidal individuals the ability to contain and bear another person's death wish without being overwhelmed and incapacitated by anxiety is imperative. What happens in therapeutic work is that "… unlike medicine, surgery, or dentistry, the mental health clinician is the instrument of care—there is no equipment failure, no pathogen, and no virus to otherwise blame. We are the instrument of care; it does not get any more personal than that" (Jobes, 2006, p. 7).

And it does not get any more important than that as suicide is often, if not always, about working through early relational failure and how that has been experienced and defended against psychologically by this particular individual. This early felt/real failure will at some level be experienced as rage against the world and all the aspects represented by this—marriage, workplace, the state, the system, the person themselves, their body. When the therapist and patient begin to make a containing space and the therapy becomes the place where this can start to be seen and get worked out in all its complexity and challenge, the need for the person to act out suicide either on themselves or on others outside the therapy diminishes—we are then in business. It may take a long time, it may mean having to endure awful times, it may mean times of great precariousness—but something becomes possible rather than impossible. The therapy comes into the place where the unbearable can just about be bearable and the urge to do something—the impulsive desire to change or alter the current unbearable situation—is slowly, fragilely, gradually replaced with the possibility of living—yes, living with hard times for sure, living with uncertainty and worry and responsibility—but living nonetheless. This is the therapeutic pursuit. Suicides rarely occur without the psychological "oomph" that is needed to overcome our natural thresholds for pain and avoidance of death. So we work to locate and galvanise that psychological oomph into something more known, more contained, and more managed. Again to quote Shneidman: "The paradox of psychotherapy is that the patient comes voluntarily to talk about things he or she doesn't ordinarily want to discuss, including those never even thought of before. The greater paradox is not that this is done, but that it turns out to be helpful" (1996, p. 141).

Many people working in today's mental health systems will be familiar with risk assessment questionnaires and forms. Please do not think I am against using these. On the contrary, how are we to know if someone is suicidal, to what degree they are suicidal, if they have ever been suicidal in the past, if we do not ask. Such risk assessment procedures are all-important. But they do not need to be overcomplicated. Also they are only as good as the person using them. A simple question about suicide may be all that is needed but it has to be asked and it has to be asked by someone who can accept the answer.

As we have noted there are many examples of coherent systems of risk assessment available to trained clinicians but it might be useful to look in more detail at one example. Some of the features of the CAMS model mentioned above, as developed by Eoin Galavan and others from the original work of David Jobes, are worth a closer look because of the strong emphasis on therapeutic engagement, relational work, and alliance. CAMS is oriented to keeping patients out of inpatient hospital settings by focusing on the direct engagement of clinical assessment and management of suicidal risk. It employs a therapeutic framework that guides suicidal people towards the goal of maintaining safety as well as problem solving the issues pertaining to their suicidality. It is fundamentally focused on developing a strong therapeutic relationship, stating: "By its very nature suicidality tends to muck up the normal processes of developing alliances because suicidal risk evokes anxiety, fear, and abject need for control and power in both sides of the clinical dyad. We believe that our ability to understand and tolerate these issues … plants the seeds of a potentially life-saving alliance" (Galavan, 2014, p. 55).

CAMS strongly emphasises the centrality of an honest therapeutic alliance made with each patient in treatment. In introducing the risk assessment tool the CAMS clinician will reflect back what the patient has told her about how bad he feels things are, maybe that he is having suicidal thoughts. In taking the patient's condition seriously—an important first step—the assessment tool can then be used to conduct a deeper and more thorough assessment of the patient's psychological state and emotional suffering and, importantly, it is completed together with the patient with his full understanding of its use and purpose— namely that it is to help identify how serious is the suicidal state and what are the treatment options.

Ongoing research from Dr Galavan and his team suggests that this sort of approach is invaluable when working with someone who is suicidal and can be utilised by any therapist of any modality. The approach emphasises the importance of trust and also therapeutic confidence. Galavan himself speaks of the need in all therapists thinking of working with suicidal people to first check that they are prepared to do this work. The clinician needs to ask themselves, "Am I prepared to do this, to be in this place with someone. Am I prepared to confront suicidality at every turn?" It is also equally important to be able to say "No". Suicide is designed to create an impact, an evocation, a reaction—it is not an act of indifference. It has the power to generate strong feelings—of fear, anger, sadness, impotence, guilt—and the therapist is not by any means immune to these feelings. On the contrary. But once a clinician is as clear as she can be that she is prepared to do this work, that she understands the parameters within which she is working, the limits in particular, and she remains fully supported by colleagues, supervisors, etc., then the work can begin and hopefully continue. Professional support, and more particularly professional clinical supervision, is essential for anyone working with suicidal patients. The work is precarious. There are endless snags and pitfalls along the way—the possibility of being made to feel too responsible, of being sucked into the damned if you do/damned if you don't dynamic, of the work being stymied by suicidal threats, to name but some. Clinical supervision is the place to process, think through, contain, and be contained in all of this complexity. I cannot emphasise the necessity of this enough and strongly suggest that no one should be working clinically with anyone who is actively suicidal unless a supervisory arrangement is fully in place.

The support and joined-up thinking between colleagues is essential too. Opportunities for collective thoughtful, reflective discussion, if there is teamwork in place, can be invaluable so that the clinician at the chalk face is not isolated and frightened or feeling too much the weight of responsibility which might mirror the world of the patient. But beware the rudimentary case conference—this is not what I mean and is often an avoidance of the level of difficulty and complexity when it comes to suicidal patients. And also beware professional one-upmanship—envy, competition, and professional territorialism—none of this is any use when we are dealing in these matters. No one model, body of knowledge, or clinical profession has dibs on understanding suicide and how to treat it. So when in doubt talk to each other, help each other out, and treat each other with respect. This will help you, the clinician, and you the patient.

Furthermore, Galavan emphasises that suicide is an interpersonal act. Talking about it has enormous power. Not talking about—refusing—remains the suicidal person's private weapon. The clinical challenges for the therapist and for others working with suicidal patients are legion—the goals of escape, peace, or payback are very beguiling for the suicidal person. If they were not he would not be suicidal. The therapist has a predominantly dual concern which mirrors the split world of the suicidal person—to continue life and to give up the suicidal fantasy but at the same time to face the return to the ordinary pain and duty of life.

What is often critical and is perhaps the defining factor between those of us who are suicidal and those who are not, and those who if they are suicidal are able to work through this, is the individual's willingness to endure pain. Shneidman quotes Robert Litman, a psychiatric colleague thus: "People commit suicide because they cannot accept their pain, because the pain does not fit in with their concept of themselves, their personal ideal. So for me the long range treatment of chronically suicidal people includes helping them change their self-concept so that they can learn to acknowledge that their pain, while unique to them, is not radically different from everyone else's pain, and their personhood is basically pretty much the same as everybody else's personhood" (1996, p. 159). It is as if suicidal people feels themselves to be particularly misunderstood, particularly challenged in a way that no one else is, that their pain is special and especially unendurable and untreatable. It almost feels grandiose—that they are special sufferers even when they are saying they are the lowest of the low. When they kill themselves there is a real intention to stay on. I read somewhere that murder is a very bad way of trying to get rid of someone—the victim will always stay around to haunt you. It is the same with suicide. It is no way to get rid of yourself! In fact I think the intention might well be to stick around, to stay in the minds and lives of others, and yet not have to do any of the sticky stuff of relationships and the hard stuff of living. Sometimes the most difficult thing to do is to endure life with all its horrible, unfair, hard, and very ordinary challenges. Sigmund Freud got it right again. In *Studies on Hysteria* he wrote of analysis that it is concerned with "… transforming your hysterical misery into common unhappiness. With a mental life that has been restored to health, you will be better armed against that unhappiness." He is not talking of promises of unadulterated joy here, just managing the everyday gristle of life!

The Canadian writer Miriam Toews has written wryly, movingly, and at times hilariously on the subject of suicide in her novel *All My Puny Sorrows*. At one point in the story, the narrator, Yoli, having just had a fairly typical and unsatisfactory conversation with a nurse in the psychiatric ward where her sister is a patient following a very serious suicide attempt, fantasises thus:

> Imagine a psychiatrist sitting down with a broken human being saying: I am here for you, I am committed to your care, I want to make you feel better, I want to return your joy to you, I don't

know how I will do it but I will find out and then I will apply one hundred percent of my abilities, my training, my compassion and my curiosity to your health—to your wellbeing, to your joy. I am here for you and I will work very hard to help you. I promise. If I fail it will be my failure, not yours. I am the professional. I am the expert. You are experiencing great pain right now and it is my job and my mission to cure you from your pain. I am absolutely committed to your care. (2014, p. 176)

Of course this is a work of fiction, although the author's own father and sister did both kill themselves. And the quote is the overwhelming wish of Yoli, sibling to a very suicidal sister, at the end of several tethers. I would not encourage *any* professional, or anyone at all for that matter, to promise to save another person's life—particularly a suicidal person's life. This we cannot and should not do. But we can and should intend to do no harm. And we are able in our society, in fact very well able, to far better resource the training of countless professional clinicians who will, because it is their job, try as hard as is possible within the limits of their capabilities, together with the suicidal person, to move that person through his unbearable pain, his un-faceable pain, and the grudge that makes him hold onto the pain. This way forward I do uphold. We certainly won't manage it all of the time, we won't even manage it most of the time, but having a good go at it, supported by society, and failing sometimes—so be it—with that we should have no problem.

CHAPTER EIGHT

Exploring the consequences

"It will generally be found that as soon as the terrors of life reach the point where they outweigh the terrors of death, a man will put an end to his life. But the terrors of death offer considerable resistance." So wrote the nineteenth-century German philosopher Arthur Schopenhauer in his essay, "On Suicide", in his *Studies in Pessimism* (1891). It seems manifestly true that because we are able to think, it follows that we are able to think of suicide as a solution to the unbearable pain or insurmountable challenges and burdens that we all face in life. However, despite our ability to contemplate suicide, not many of us actually go on to kill ourselves. As we have seen, the conditions that lead someone to take their own life are far from simple, straightforward, or understandable; nor is suicide easy to carry out. As Schopenhauer went onto say, "Suicide is the destruction of the body; and a man shrinks from that because his body is the manifestation of life." In some ways Schopenhauer is echoing Freud's puzzle over the pleasure principle—how, if we are driven to pursue our needs and our pleasures, do we understand the drive to destruction? In understanding suicide as both an act of the self and against the self, as an act of destruction turned against the self, we can begin to understand its hold over us. We have faced the reality of suicide throughout the ages and across cultures and enough of us continue to die by suicide for it to be worthy of our inquiry. Despite out best efforts, and some not so good efforts, suicide is determinedly with us. We do not seem to be able to stay its hand.

Suicide leaves its mark on those left behind in a particular, peculiar, and devastating way. This is part of the drama of the act. Thus the world of suicide is peopled by those who cannot "get over" the death of their loved one by suicide. They set up charities, they start support groups, they visit the grave, they write books (!), or, as a study in absolute denial, they never talk about it at all. Suicide has a particular power. This is part of the intention, albeit unconscious, of the suicidal person—to leave behind the struggle and pain of their life, through their death, but leave it for others to wrestle with and puzzle over forever. Those who are bereaved through suicide are left constantly questioning: "Why did they do it?" "What was the matter?" "What was so wrong?" "Why didn't they tell me?" If murder is no way to get rid of someone else, suicide is no way to be forgotten!

The Russian poet Boris Pasternak wrote of the bankruptcy of the suicidal person thus:

> A man who decides to commit suicide puts a full stop to his being. He turns his back on his past, he declares himself bankrupt and his memories to be unreal. They can no longer help or save him, he has put himself beyond their reach. The continuity of his inner life is broken, his personality is at an end. And perhaps what finally makes him kill himself is not the firmness of his resolve but the unbearable quality of this anguish which belongs to no one, of this suffering in the absence of the sufferer, of this waiting which is empty because life has stopped and can no longer fill it. (1959, p. 92)

Here Pasternak captures beautifully what we might call in psychoanalytic parlance the power of projection and projective identification; of evacuation. The person who dies by suicide is thinking only about escape, about themselvess and about the satisfaction of some fantasy realised. They have broken their connection with the continuity of life, and consequently the continuity of relationship with others; but the others who remain alive after his death have to face the consequences of the unconscious aspect of the act; they do have continuity and they receive the full onslaught of the accusation left behind: "Why were you not enough for me?"

Sadly this is not an accusation made against a real Other—it is one which whistles in the wind. As Pasternak says it belongs to no one. But this is small consolation for those who are on the receiving end of it. Those bereaved by suicide will feel it as a shocking, numbing, decimating, fatal blow to them. They are almost inevitably going to receive the accusation, at least in part, as if it *does* belong to them. If a suicide note is left it can sometimes spell out this accusation fully or disingenuously.

As we have learnt, the actual act of suicide can take many forms. Some people take themselves off without seeming to say a word, disappear for days, and then their body is found many miles from their home. Others make quite sure that their death has an impact. They hang themselves in the hallway of the family home; gas themselves in the garage; jump from the highest building on the university campus; throw themselves in front of a busy commuter train. Sometimes this is deeply personal—antagonistic, violent, and deliberately aimed at their nearest and dearest; sometimes it is very public and aimed at everyone. Each act of suicide will have its own nuances and twists and will leave its particular mark on those left behind. It is not unknown for a suicide to take place when others are carrying on their everyday business in the same house. Whatever the circumstances, and the deeply rooted enactment, the legacy of suicide is far reaching.

Those bereaved by suicide will have certain things in common with those bereaved by any death but there are other aspects of being bereaved by suicide which are unique. As with all deaths the bereaved are faced with the huge and immediate loss of the person, and then with the long road ahead without them as this loss becomes permanent. They will go through a range of emotions and states of feeling from shock, numbness, grief, pain, sadness, anger, and guilt. These latter emotions of guilt and anger can be common in many reactions to a death but among those who have lost someone to suicide they are often intense and long lasting. Anger can often be particularly hard to feel because guilt gets in the way. The self-berating questioning the bereaved are left with can be endless: "I should have done more." "If only I had known how they were feeling." "Why didn't they tell me?" "I can't bear to think about how they felt and that they were on their own." Suicide is devious, complex, contradictory, often hidden, and bewildering. It leaves us all questioned and questioning.

The bereaved face additional difficulties beyond so-called "normal" bereavement. As with any sudden death there are no farewells. A suicide note can seem as if it is a kind of farewell, it may even contain some sentiment of a goodbye, but it is usually a very mixed blessing to be on the receiving end of such a note. In his analysis of suicide notes held in the Los Angeles County Coroner's Office, Shneidman found that for the most part they expressed the excessive psychological pain of the deceased. In other words they were largely introspective. This bears out Pasternak's point above—the disconnect with the Other, with relationship, and with continuity of life. The notes left rarely speak to the relatives left behind. Instead they speak of the person himself and of his internal suffering. If suicidal notes do directly refer to others they are often vengeful or indirectly guilt inducing. I was involved peripherally with the suicide of a colleague many years ago who sent more than twenty notes to a range of family members, friends, and colleagues. All of them pretty much contained the same entreaty, repeated several times in different ways: "Please do not feel guilty. This is not your fault. Please have a happy life without me. You couldn't have done any more." When I read these notes I remember feeling enraged on their behalves—if the recipients were not already feeling guilty about the death before they got the note then they were certainly being encouraged to feel so on receipt! A case of protesting rather too much.

Many people who have suffered the death by suicide of a close friend or relative may well have been involved with the person's mental and emotional struggle for months or even years. The struggle may have caused disruption and distress for some time within a family or relationship. When the person takes her own life the bereaved may well be left with confusing feelings among which could well be relief. This is a very hard emotion to admit to in the face of the death of someone close. But nevertheless it is important to be able to acknowledge it, if it is felt, alongside the loss, because in some very real sense a long-term incomprehensible burden has now been lifted.

Others can get caught up in a sort of tussle, a power struggle, a tug of war almost, between the suicidal person's determination to die and their own determination to stop him. In such a way the bereaved may well be left with feelings that they have failed. I would argue that in such cases they were getting caught up in the suicidal person's own split, carrying for him the part that still wanted to live. It is hugely difficult to work this out at the time and to have the insight or courage to step a little further away so that this collusion can be challenged.

Furthermore, in taking himself out of the picture completely the suicidal person leaves the bereaved without any chance of an end note
themselves, a farewell, or at least some chance to reconcile themselves
to the death. This is of course the case with any sudden death but with
suicide the suddenness has an added twist as it leaves the bereaved with
a big pile of unanswered or perhaps unasked questions—unfinished
business in no small measure and no chance of working this out with the
departed. "The most important informant [about what was the matter]
can no longer be questioned" (Stengel, 1965, p. 103). Continuing the
search for answers goes some way to understanding the proliferation of
suicidal charities set up by the bereaved which make such an important
contribution to gaining insight and providing much-needed resources
for the suicidal. But however helpful these associations are, they may in
some way prevent the acceptance that the causes of any suicidal event
can never really be fully fathomed. Sadly, those who are bereaved by
suicide have in front of them a long, lonely, and hard journey to accept-
ing that they will never know all the answers to "Why?".

The other notable difference when someone dies by suicide, as
compared to a natural or accidental death, is that when a suicide is
discovered or suspected the death becomes a matter of public investigation and legal inquiry. This inevitably has an immediate impact
on how the death is experienced by the bereaved. In some cases evidence will have to be gathered and removed from the family home.
This will include the suicide note(s) if any have been left. All this legal
and investigative procedure can feel like a huge intrusion and disturbance to what might otherwise be a private, deeply intimate experience in the first instance. In all cases of suicide there will be a coroner's
inquest, and family members, lovers, close friends, etc. may be asked
to attend as witnesses or want to attend in the hope of gaining more
clarity. Coroner's courts are formal places and the coroner has a legal
role to play in deciding the verdict of the death. For most people this
may be the first time they have been in any sort of court and they will
not know what to expect, how things will be conducted, what they
will hear, or who will be there. When my sister died the inquest was
heard at St Pancras Coroner's Court in London. I was called as a witness as I had been in daily contact with Olivia right up to her death.
In fact I believe I was the last person to speak to her, on the telephone,
in the early evening of the night she died. I was twenty-six years old

at the time and had no familiarity with the workings of the law or the courts. I had no idea what to expect and could barely put one foot in front of the other at the time let alone speak coherently. The first question the coroner asked me when I entered the witness stand was, "How long have you known the deceased?" This still bewilders me—it was such a pointless, bureaucratic question. I was my sister's sister! I remember not being able to think at all, not actually knowing what the right answer was—was it my age or her age? I felt completely paralysed and couldn't think of the right answer. In the end I blurted out "All my life," ... then mumbled "twenty-six years." To this day this is the only thing I can really remember from the whole experience. I am sure the coroner was a thoughtful and sensitive person but procedurally it seemed remote. Probably because it was—utterly remote from what I was going through.

Another more ugly aspect of death by suicide is that when a suicide occurs we are often exposed to the darker, prurient side of human interest. While the courts are formal and necessary legal places they are also open to the public, and to press reporters. The *Hackney Gazette*— never known for its understatement—reported my sister's death in three columns interspaced with two, single word subheads: "Actress" and "Blonde". I shall leave the reader to ponder the point, or the value, of those particular choices of subheadings! Suffice to say the insinuations are glaring. Since then I am glad to say that a lot of sensible and responsible work has been done between the Press Complaints Commission, broadcasters in general, and those working on suicide prevention to forestall ill-informed reporting of suicide. It is deeply distressing enough for anyone to be bereaved by suicide—it is a private and shocking tragedy—without being subjected to prying eyes and sensational and inaccurate public reporting. In the case of so-called copycat or cluster suicides (see Chapter Six, p. 71), a particularly nasty twist in suicide epistemology, inaccurate and gratuitously detailed press reporting can be downright reckless.

Thus the quality and type of press reporting on suicide in these days of multiple media can be hugely significant and needs to be particularly responsible as opposed to sensational or dramatic. It also needs to be sensitive and timely in order to give the bereaved the space and privacy they need. The Press Complaints Commission's editors' code contains detailed guidance on taste and decency, on avoiding the publication of gratuitous pictures or material, and on intrusion into grief and shock.

In June 2006, the guidance was tightened to include a new subclause, reading: "When reporting suicide, care should be taken to avoid excessive detail about the method used." This change was made in response to evidence from the Samaritans and other groups about the triggers for copycat suicides. However, most interest groups do not call for an overall ban on the reporting of suicides but wish to encourage responsible reporting rather than no reporting. There are benefits to publishing well informed articles which focus attention and resources, and encourage greater understanding of its complexity. This all helps to reduce the fear and most significantly in the case of cluster suicides, discourage the drama. Thus any reporting of a suicide should not be romanticised, suicide notes should not be disclosed, and excessive detail should be avoided. Sensitive and sensible reporting can help by dispelling common misconceptions about suicide, such as that people who attempt to take their own lives are beyond help or, conversely, need not be taken seriously. Better informed journalism that encourages more of us to think properly about suicide, and how we might help or get help ourselves, is to be encouraged.

Another area of distinction for those bereaved by suicide is how they themselves are responded to after the death. Like anyone suffering a bereavement the reactions of those around us can be helpful and supportive, but not always. Not everyone is comfortable with death and with responding to it. With suicide this is all the more problematic. When the death is by suicide we find ourselves unable or unwilling to offer "normal" responses, as if the suicide has taken death to an even more fearful or unacceptable place. The bereaved may find contact with the very people they need support from fraught, uncomfortable, and distancing. It is as if bereavement by suicide is contaminated by the same socially unacceptable quality of suicide itself, and the bereaved are exposed in some measure to the same isolation, disavowal, and distancing that the suicidal themselves experience. Because we are unsure of how we should respond, avoidance is commonly chosen as the preferred solution. This is often a mutual problem. The bereaved do not know how to talk about the death by suicide. They may feel very reluctant to talk about the cause of death; it is not uncommon for families to lie about the details and to make up some other cause of death which they think is more acceptable. This can get particularly complicated if the bereaved feel they are in some way to blame—again something which is far from uncommon with suicide. In which case they may fear and feel the avoidance of others is to be expected, that it is what they deserve—they may even encourage it by their own behaviour. Their guilt and shame will get in the way of them getting the support they need themselves. Families may also fall out among themselves after a suicidal death. Some will have been more involved and feel others did not help; others will blame the deceased and may avoid collective grieving. In turn these differences may lead to further family friction.

Some will have been the ones who coped, who did everything they could for the suicidal person, who held others together. For these people, getting help for themselves after the death will be extremely hard. Relinquishing the benefits of the coping role and admitting their own vulnerability and need, as well as feeling they have failed, will make it harder for them. They may also harbour unconscious resentment at the dead person for not being saved by all that they tried to do for him, and at others for not knowing that they need help themselves.

I was fortunate when my sister died to have a particularly strong friendship group and good enough relations with my other siblings. I remember asking one friend to tell the others in our social group, and to tell them truthfully, about when and how Olivia died, so that when I next felt able to go out with them the details of Olivia's death would be held and known in some way without my needing to go over all the details. He did this for me and the others responded well. They were a good lot and I am still very close to several of these friends to this day. I don't think that is a coincidence. In contrast, in the days leading up to her funeral, while staying with my mother, I overheard some of mother's friends and neighbours suggesting to her that Olivia may have taken too many pills by accident. At the time of her death she was very thin and they suggested that, due to her tiny frame and because of the strong drugs she was on, "She probably got confused and took too many for her body to manage," They meant well and were trying to support my mother. Also I suspect this may have been what my mother preferred to hear—she was utterly out of her depth with it all. But I remember feeling absolutely furious at the time. Unfair of me really as they were trying their best, and of course the person I was really furious with was dead. But all this illustrates just how difficult it is to respond, to get the right touch, the right words, the right amount of sensitivity, the right amount of space for the particular person who has been bereaved, since each in our own way will be dealing with the death differently and for different reasons. We will each have had, like my mother and myself, a different relationship with the dead person and will feel the death contextually, dynamically, in very different ways. Perhaps this is all an indication of the only thing we do know—there is no right way. People will differ in how they feel and what they are left with. All we can do, all of us, is allow those who are bereaved by a suicide to lead the way and to stand alongside them while they go through their pain in their own time and in their own way.

Certainly in the UK there is plenty of help and support available for those bereaved by suicide. This is important to consider since people who have lost family members by suicide are at greater risk of death by suicide themselves. For children this can be for two main reasons—first, that their parent has modelled a way out of life's difficulties by his or her own suicide. For the offspring it can then become an internalised option. Second, they have experienced a severe loss at a time when they are particularly in need of parenting, which is a major abandonment for them. They may feel that the parent has left them because they are not important enough for the parent to stay alive. This can take hold over many years, grow deep and hidden roots, and thus can be subtly pernicious. It is always advisable when working psychotherapeutically or within the psychiatric services or in general practice to take a detailed history of family life when first seeing a patient in order to ascertain if there have been any suicides in the family, even if suicide does not seem to present itself at all in the patient.

The final thing to emphasise in exploring the consequences of suicide is that a suicide, although a highly individual act, takes place in the context of relationship. Current research shows that individuals who remember their parents as rejecting, overcritical, overexacting, or cold are at greater risk of suicide ideation and behaviour because such experiences predispose the person to intense self-criticism and perfectionism. These are factors associated with suicidal ideation and behaviour. Early difficult, overprotective, or disrupted attachment to parents—through actual abandonment and neglect or perceived abandonment—can lead later to insecure attachment which is also linked to suicide in both adolescents and adults. Insecurely attached individuals have difficulty with separation and constantly seek reassurance and support in anticipation of rejection. This can result in a cycle of low self-esteem and increased need for interpersonal contact which in turn leads to experiences of rejection and feeds the feelings that "I am unloveable/not good enough". There is a noticeable self-punitive, distrustful style of relating that characterises such a person.

Such self-critical perfectionism appears as an overly critical feeling about one's own behaviour, an inability to derive satisfaction from even a successful performance, and chronic concerns about what others think of you, how you compare to others, etc. All are highly problematic factors associated with suicide. Sadly these traits can develop from the most innocent and well intentioned parental and cultural expectations. We only need to look at the current madness in the school system in the UK where it now seems increasingly impossible to get less than best. A's have been regraded as A* and then A**. What is wrong with a C if that is what you are capable of? It is incredibly important to be able to do less well, to try things and not succeed, to be frustrated and to fail. We need to offer our young people the most important experience of all—that even if they do not succeed, even if they are not top or the best, they will be loved and tolerated. Life will always throw new and difficult things at us all and we must be able to believe that how we manage these is the real test of a life. That our sense of self is not conditional on how well we gratify parental or society's narcissism and fear. We should not think we have to be perfect, or fear that the world will abandon us if we are not. I have spent the last few years training in working with suicidality in universities throughout the UK, and what I have heard from tutors and counsellors working in these settings regarding perfectionism has concerned me greatly.

In cases of actual childhood abandonment, abuse, and awful neglect, the rage and feelings of despair and hate turned against the self can of course be lethal. In such cases these experiences are known, clear, and real, but funnily enough are often survivable. But with suicide the assaults on the self are often grown from merely perceived slights, or accidents of fate if you like. The middle child, commonplace sibling rivalry, the child born when parents are not getting on, the child born to a bereaved or ill mother, or the child who is inadvertently or unconsciously scapegoated by the family—any of these circumstances of birth can breed dangerous and damaging introjects which then fester like untreated infected wounds and become self-fulfilling, self-critical, damaging feelings in the person concerned. Sometimes families perpetuate very subtle, often unwitting scapegoating or labelling to defend themselves from differences and conflicts that are in fact necessary, inevitable, and natural in any family. This can then give rise to all sorts of internalised bad feelings in the receiver. However, we are not in fact all the same, nor can we be what our parents want us to be to fulfil their own unmet or unknown needs. Sometimes the child feels herself or himself to be different from the rest of the family—the exception as Freud called it. It is all these complexities, nuances, and other mysterious elements that make up how our lives unfold, not just external circumstances and genetics. How we are done to by others and then by ourselves, once we are born, is crucial as to how we manage the vicissitudes of life once they come—and come they will for sure.

We are all, including the suicidal amongst us, individuals, but we live in the context of relationship. The suicidal are often acting out a role assigned to them and taken on by them in early childhood even if they are well into older adulthood. No wonder they leave an indelible mark for the people left behind. For those left behind the loss felt by suicide can seem irredeemable, something which they will never understand and from which they cannot move beyond, or it can herald a turning point, a point of important insight into damage that can be tempered over time, albeit not overnight. Pain, sadness, guilt, rage, terrible fear, and vulnerability are felt but so too is the possibility of potential, of seeing things differently. A suicide very close to you can be a signal to try to manage difficult things differently yourself; it can become an opportunity to make sense of the world differently if you can. A death by suicide can make you face something—at the time you may not know what it is—and it can help you respond to things differently in the future, to face damage in yourself. It can also help you appreciate that you cannot fix everything and that everything that happens is not about you.

CHAPTER NINE

Final thoughts

Any discussion about suicide is going to be difficult. Suicide is never going to be a neutral or mild subject. Suicide is about extreme feeling or feeling extreme. It is a strong response to life and, consequently, it arouses strong responses in others. Suicide is "over the top". It is out of proportion—it is "*out–rage–ous*". Suicide is not a proportional response to anything. It is a rageful act about something felt to be too much. It is a desperate act of escape, of getting away from all that is felt to be unbearable, unmanageable, and unfair. Suicide is an unbearable solution to unbearable feeling. It leaves behind something unbearable for the bereaved.

However, we do talk of rational suicide, by which we appear to mean a suicide that makes sense to and about the person involved, and presumably to others. The arguments for rational suicide are supported by the notion of autonomy, namely that we must be able to act according to our own desires and beliefs without interference from others. Following on from such ideas the right to die is seen as an expression of autonomy, in extremis: we have the right to choose the time and manner of our dying. Arguments in support of rational suicide also rely on the belief that an individual has the ability to make a rational assessment of their utility or "good" in living, of the quality of their life as opposed to ending their life. Suicide in this way is seen as a way of deciding to cease painful and hopeless disease, feelings, pain, or circumstances. However, this reasoning is based on an assumption that autonomy, as the exercise of independent thought, independently derived, free from culture, society, relationship, psychological turf, etc., is possible. But as we have seen throughout this book, to be able to conclude that an act or intention of suicide is reasonable, rational, is not a straightforward matter. Also, since the experience of being dead is entirely unknown—regardless of any religious belief—it is highly questionable whether it is possible to "know" what the outcome will be. So the question which remains in my mind is not "Are there any conditions in which suicide is a reasonable response?", but rather "Why are so many suicides carried out with respect to what are in fact inevitable and ordinary life experiences (albeit tough ones—loss, deprivation, shame, isolation)?" Why do some of us manage life, with all its vicissitudes, and others do not? Suicide, it seems, contrary to appearances, is largely an internal problem not an external one. The concept of suicide as understandable within the context of the individual's psyche is more meaningful than any concept of it being a rational act. And it is within an understanding of the person's internal world that the clue to helping a suicidal person ultimately lies.

I think the challenge of working with someone who is suicidal, of helping them, is actually about not colonising them or their suicidality. By which I mean not to try to make them see sense from a point of view, your point of view or that of society, to see that life *must* be worth it. But rather to act in a way that allows them to occupy the territory they need to, which in this case is the territory of suicide—no matter how harrowing this is for them and for you. In a way the potential helper needs to be saying: "I am not promoting any desire or aim of my own here—I am interested only in you and in your psychic pain, in knowing it, in bearing it, and in relieving it if possible." This then makes the possibility of their working out their pain more likely and refuses the seduction of re-enacting any such earlier lack of attunement or impinging, thwarted experience. In contrast, suicide strategy documents, risk assessment protocols, suicide reduction targets, the language of zero tolerance, "no suicide" contracts, while conceived of with the best of intentions, are all acts of colonisation in some sense. They will be felt as pressures by those providing services and possibly as grave misunderstandings by the suicidal person.

The clinical and personal challenge to anyone working with a suicidal patient is also magnified because of how beguiling suicide is. If it were not so there would not be suicidal acts carried out daily. We have to recognise how for the suicidal person continuance with life is commensurate with facing something felt to be intolerable; a life to be lived that they may be unwilling to endure. Shneidman reflects on this, saying, "What is critical is the individual's unwillingness to endure pain." And he continues: "In suicide there is often the feeling that one's pain is somehow special and greater than the pain and suffering of others, making it unendurable in a special way—bordering on a feeling of grandiosity" (1996, pp. 159–160). Here Shneidman is touching on something vital in understanding suicide and also very challenging to the clinician: how to remain understanding of that individual's psychic pain and their experience of it and not be dismissive in the face of what might seem disproportional. For some people the most difficult thing is to choose an ordinary life when tasked to do so with all its inevitable challenges, disappointments, and hardships. The hard work is to root out where this sense of special pain arose and what the wished for other/ideal life reveals. Simply put, offering a non-judgemental and reflective presence can sometimes be the most helpful and immediate action for the isolated and desperate suicidal person.

Another aspect which is immensely challenging to the clinician or helper is the closed mindedness of the suicidal person. They have reached, and seem determined to remain in, a state of tunnel vision, of dictatorship, of totalitarianism of the mind. This sense of entrapment, of a thought or state of mind that you are stuck in and cannot get out of, is redolent of the suicidal mind. The suicidal person is saying, "The *only* thing I can do is to kill myself." In the face of such entrenchment it is sometimes immensely hard to introduce any other perception, feeling state, or capacity to think. To quote Shneidman again: "Every single instance of suicide is an action by the dictator or emperor of your mind. But in every case of suicide the person is getting bad advice from a part of that mind … in no position to serve the person's best long range interests. … suicide is not the thing to do when you are disturbed and your thinking is constricted" (1996, pp. 165–166). The reason for this absolute closed mindedness is because what needs to be examined, what is underneath, what seems impossible to face, may be very unpalatable for the person concerned, but absolutely necessary if his life is going to be saved. One of the key phrases of Shneidman's is the "long range interests" of the person. Much of what has to be done for someone who is actively, chronically suicidal combines relieving shortterm and immediate pain, pressure, fear, danger, parlous circumstances, etc., but at the same time gently enabling him to unravel the complexity and trauma that has brought him to this state. The latter intervention is a long-range aim needing long-term input. Suicidality is rarely removed over-night, although a threat of immediate suicidal action must of course be attended to in the here and now. In other words when working with someone who is actively suicidal we are required to deal with the sub-soil (long-term intervention) *and* the immediacy of the pull towards death (here and now intervention).

And where might such responses best be found? Certainly, suicidal people need help of one kind or another although they may not seek it or want to face this. Psychological therapies can be the best course of action for those who are able and willing to access such treatment and they offer the long-range opportunity that is needed for proper and safe examination, exhumation, and ultimately, psychological change. As discussed in previous chapters, suicidality lends itself to thorough exploration and to the examination of unconscious mechanisms at play in the suicidal fantasy. But sometimes the feeling of crisis, isolation, and despair is too great and the unconscious ambivalence and unacknowl-edged anger act against people who are actively suicidal accessing such treatment.

In the UK the Samaritans offer a service that is available 365 days a year, 24 hours a day, to anyone who is emotionally troubled, in despair, or who feels isolated and suicidal. Overall they emphasise their capacity to listen and volunteers are trained to focus on exploring the caller's thoughts and feelings without judgement. Most important, they don't tell the caller what to do and they do not give advice or their own opinions. In a way this is an attempt not to colonise the caller. As their website states, "We won't talk about ourselves, even if you ask us to. We're there to give you time, space and support—you don't need to ask how we are, or give us time in return. We don't impose any personal attitudes or beliefs on you. We're not religious."

Samaritans also maintain absolute confidentiality of all suicidal callers and they maintain this position throughout the organisation. This means they are very widely used by all manner of people who are in various states of mind and condition, from the lonely, the muddled and con-fused, the frightened, the guilty, the despairing, to the actively suicidal.

Their popularity and the demographic diversity of callers to the Samaritans is largely due to the fact that the volunteers offer such a profoundly safe space to all callers and an opportunity to be heard in a completely non-judgemental way with no expectations of outcome. They also allow what needs to be articulated by the caller regardless of whether this seems to be at odds with conventions or social norms. This cannot be valued highly enough in this precarious territory. In their own simple way they probably do more to prevent suicides than any other of our highly regulated medical and evidence based interventions.

Along with health based services, psychological therapies, and the Samaritans, there are other very helpful initiatives in the UK for those who are suicidal. I highlight these in particular because I believe they respond to the precariousness of suicide, by offering a place of safety, and to the need for a non-judgemental response, both of which are vital in suicide prevention. The Maytree Foundation is one such organisation based in London. Maytree describes itself as a "sanctuary for the suicidal". It is a registered charity which aims to support people in suicidal crisis with the emphasis on it being a non-medical setting. It states on its website that it "aims to alleviate suffering and help people in suicidal crisis to re-engage with life and to restore hope". Unusually Maytree offers overnight respite and accommodation for those who are suicidal. People can self-refer or be introduced by friends, relatives, or anyone wanting to help. The Maytree Suicide Respite Centre is the only place of its kind in the UK and fills a gap in services between the medical support of the NHS, the independent psychological therapies, and the helplines and drop-in centres of the voluntary sector. They offer a free four-night/five-day stay, and the opportunity to be befriended and heard in complete confidence, without judgement, and with compassion and warmth. The staff at Maytree are not in the business of long-term therapeutic or psychiatric treatment but instead, importantly, they offer an immediate and safe place, a chance to rest completely, at that particularly lethal time when to act on suicide is at its most pressing. In some ways this is an opportunity to have the relief of escape, albeit for a few days only, without actually having to die in the process. They describe their provision thus: "… as an opportunity for rest and reflection, and an opportunity to stay in a calm, safe and relaxed environment. We can support four 'guests' at a time. The service runs 24 hours a day, 365 days a year." To quote again from its website: "Our warm and friendly volunteers and staff team spend up to 77 hours with each guest over their stay, giving them the opportunity to talk through their fears, thoughts and troubles." During their stay "guests" are encouraged to discuss how to access further support from other agencies, psychotherapy, counselling, etc., and also identify what else might be helpful—housing, financial or other practical support—and to put in place other aspects which might make their lives safer and easier. However, Maytree is but one tiny organisation, located in a very ordinary house in a suburban London street. It seems to me there is no reason why more such centres cannot be established at little cost, to respond in an essentially human way to a human need. Such centres could be a vital lifeline to many people confronting their suicidal feelings in isolation.

Just such a new initiative, similar to Maytree but with notable differences, is in the process of development. Clare Milford Haven and her ex-husband Nick Wentworth-Stanley set up the James Wentworth-Stanley Memorial Fund (JWSMF) in memory of their son James, who took his own life in 2006. Up till now the JWSMF has primarily been a grant-giving body, promoting training and research into the causes and prevention of suicide among young people. But its new aspiration is to set up crisis centres, to be known as James Places, that can provide counselling and psychotherapy services for the suicidal. The mission statement explains: "James Place exists to help adults who are in crisis, by providing quick and free access to therapy and support." The hope is to be the first crisis day centre in the United Kingdom for working age adults (over sixteen) in severe emotional distress with suicidal ideation and to develop multiple centres in the UK. The following tenets with respect to the philosophy of James Place centres are cited:

- Caring for their patients
- Not judging their patients, but offering practical advice
- Maintaining patients' confidentiality
- Operational independence from the NHS
- Providing emotional support in a peaceful, non-clinical environment
- Working consultatively and collaboratively
- Financial transparency.

The centres will open six days a week, Monday—Saturday, and offer an initial assessment followed by eight to ten sessions of psychotherapy provided by registered psychotherapists. The aim is to provide expert immediate face-to-face support to alleviate the feelings of suicidal ideation, with follow-up support. They will not be walk-in centres—instead patients will be referred from healthcare professionals, partner organisations, friends, and relatives, and will be offered an initial telephone screening in order to assess that they meet the criteria of the service. Ideally James Places will be located separately from, but relatively near to, an A & E hospital to encourage access and collaboration. As I write discussions are being held in Liverpool for the site of the first James Place.

What both Maytree and James Place, together with the Pieta House project in Ireland, all build on is the idea that safe, compassionate, and therapeutic intervention with people with suicidal ideation is of great importance. Suicide is not an inevitable outcome. As we have seen, people considering suicide have doubts about it; it is an ambivalent act. Therefore good, informed suicide prevention becomes crucial. However, inpatient acute mental health services are often unsuitable for patients who are suicidal—suicidal people are not necessarily ill—and such services often fail to address the individual needs of the patient/person or provide a safe and therapeutic environment. Inpatient facilities can replicate a chaotic and frightening internal feeling and also increase fears of death. However, at the same time, home treatment is not always appropriate or accessible, particularly at times of acute crisis. Places such as Maytree, James Place, and Pieta House can offer much of what is needed when a person is actively suicidal, namely safety, containment, respite, and therapeutic understanding—which can then be built on once the immediate crisis is lessened. Interestingly, as interventions, they also all aim to act and position themselves (geographically as well as symbolically) somewhere between medical care and human care. It is worth noting that James Place seeks to locate the actual buildings for the centres somewhere near to, but not within hospital grounds. This to me represents quite an important statement about suicidality itself: that it is not a medical condition but a psychological condition, a state of mind. But at the same time the need for medical intervention cannot be ruled out along with other external, practical interventions (financial, welfare, housing, etc.). So the way ahead may well lie in making interventions for the suicidal much more collaborative and immediate (in relation to suicide acts), involving different resources and finding creative and careful ways to traverse all manner of systemic and organisational barriers which can sometimes feel insurmountable, often unhelpful, and, more important, often parallel and mimic the suicidal person's internal confusion, fears, and defences. Indeed, the establishment of such centres near to A & Es is itself a stroke of creative thinking. As well as providing the necessary neutrality and calm for the containment of the suicidal person's most destructive feelings, they would also be well placed to offer therapeutic assessment *as soon as possible* after a suicide has been attempted—this offers an early opportunity for the therapist to be "... included in the original chaos and to receive the raw projections immediately ... the need to repeat the suicidal act may then be reduced. Once the process of repression and denial has started it will be necessary for the patient to recreate their same sadomasochistic relationship with the same vulnerability to suicide" (Campbell & Hale, 1991, p. 304). If therapy can begin as soon as possible after such a suicidal act is attempted or seriously contemplated there is likely to be much more direct access to the person's emotions and, more important, their unconscious suicidal fantasy. Therapy can then continue and in so doing retain access to the unconscious within a safe and established therapeutic relationship at the same time as other day-to-day help/medical treatment can also be provided, if and wherever necessary. The general aim will be to establish a supportive enough matrix of involvement and treatment—which could be a combination of therapy, medical treatment, and welfare help—for as long as necessary. What these alternative crisis and respite centres such as Maytree and James Place are able to offer, which is potentially life-saving where suicide is concerned, is treatment within a time frame *that the person themselves can manage* and that does not play into their excessive vulnerability to rejection or into their capacity to split services (and people) into good and bad. Offering an appointment from a busy A & E, with an unnamed medical psychologist or psychiatrist in an outpatient clinic, days or even weeks hence, or organising a referral back to a mental health crisis team or GP care, will just not do justice to what is needed in the acute phase. A suicidal person is hell-bent on rejecting help and killing off the good as well as believing he or she is all bad and utterly rejectable. As Campbell and Hale suggest, "A central belief of the suicidal person is that he has the capacity to kill off all of his good objects. To offer him an appointment beyond his own time span, or with a person whom he has not met, will be perceived as both further rejection and confirmation of his belief in his own destructiveness" (1991, p. 305).

And what of our collective, general awareness of suicide? If initiatives such as those described above are to help prevent suicide, all of us need to be much better informed about suicide so that if needs be we can act on behalf of ourselves and others but also so that we are able to think about suicide and our responses to it in a reasonable and reflective way. Recently I attended a speed awareness course—this might seem a bit of a non sequitur at this junction but there is a point to my musings! Like many people I had been caught by a speed trap in a 40 mph zone doing a few miles over the limit. I was offered the option of doing a speed awareness course instead of a fine and points on my licence, so I opted for it. I admit I was unenthusiastic, feeling it would all be rather a bore and there were a million other things I would rather do than sit in a stuffy room and listen to someone unimaginatively telling me all there was to know about statistics on speeding—not my idea of a day well spent! But I was pleasantly surprised. The course was really good. It was well run by two rather droll and very well informed trainers. We were given lots of information interspersed with videos, clips, little tests on speeding knowledge, and very dry jokes! But notwithstanding the quality of the training—and readers may have their own very different experiences of such training—what stayed with me the most was how, in just four hours, my whole perception of the dangers of low level speeding was substantially changed and improved. And I think the training achieved this for all twenty or so of the other attendees. So this got me thinking. In 2013 there were 1713 RTA (road traffic accident) deaths in Great Britain. In the same year there were 6110 deaths by suicide in Great Britain—over three times as many. What if we were to introduce something similar—suicide awareness training—for anyone who was interested or directly or indirectly affected by suicide. Of course the tricky part is not designing the course but getting anyone to attend—suicide is not a great crowd-pleaser and making it mandatory would be completely counterproductive. Unlike with speeding awareness courses where mandatory attendance is extremely effective and can be made so because the alternative is a fine and penalty points on your licence, there could be no requirements or enforced incentives for attendance. And in any case who would we mandate to attend— those who are suicidal, those who might be suicidal, the bereaved, the professionals …? Nevertheless the idea of raising awareness about suicide in very simple ways, not just for professionals, is I think something to work on together. However, even this simple idea is not so simple on further reflection. Suicide is essentially a subversive act and consequently awareness, if we are not too careful, can drift into permissiveness. In some types of suicidal behaviour this could push the suicidal person into more transgressive and darker territory.

In fact there is no right or wrong position to adopt in relation to suicide. Suicidal thinking is experienced by all sorts of people in all sorts of different ways and at varying times in their lives. Sometimes the suicidal thoughts are acted on and sometimes not. For some people having suicide in mind is a long-term position which actually helps to keep them alive—the notion that they can die sustains them in living. For others it appears to come out of the blue and takes hold in a furiously fast-acting, dangerously seductive form, blinding the mind to thinking in any other way. For others still, suicide is just there, nudging away, picking away, irritating just under the surface, causing them to fall in and out of suicide attempts and self-destructive acts. So perhaps what is most useful when thinking about suicide is to remain open and also to remain in a state of useful and questioning doubt and uncertainty. Here I am reminded of the poet Keats's marvellous entreaty to us all to celebrate the state, the art, of "not knowing" of that which he called "negative capability". He wrote of this thus: "… and it struck me what quality went to form a Man of Achievement especially in Literature & which Shakespeare possessed so enormously—I mean *Negative Capability*, that is when a man is capable of being in uncertainties, Mysteries, doubts, without any irritable reaching after fact & reason" (Rollins, 1958, pp. 193–194). Although Keats was mostly writing here about the experience and achievement of capturing something beautiful and mysterious in literature rather than seeking after facts, I think the same plea can be extended to other considerations where seeking after facts actually gets in the way of remaining receptive to something not easily known or understood but simply felt or experienced. This chimes with the psychoanalyst Wilfred Bion who wrote of the psychoanalyst in *Seminar in Paris*,

> It is very important to be aware that you may never be satisfied with your analytic career if you feel that you are restricted to what is narrowly called a "scientific" approach. You will have to be able to have a chance of feeling that the interpretation you give is a beautiful one, or that you get a beautiful response from the patient. This aesthetic element of beauty makes a very difficult situation tolerable. (1978, in *The Complete Works of Wilfred Bion, Volume IX*, 2014)

Of course when working with someone who is suicidal it is a stretch to think we may be able to find something beautiful—but, and it is an important but, we may be reaching in the right direction if we let this be the way and, sometimes even if the interpretation is about something awful, the connection it makes to the patient can itself be beautiful in Bion's terms. Making the connection with the patient at a time when they believe no Other is available to be connected with, and no Other would want to connect with them, is in itself a tremendous thing. Perhaps this is what suicide awareness really needs to embrace.

We are never going to stop all suicides. Suicide is shocking, disturbing, and horribly distressing, but not surprising. Given the assault course that is life and how difficult it is for us to manage it, how much we all push our more difficult experiences and feelings into the unconscious, it is not a surprise that this internal conflict can finally get the better of so many of us. Suicide in a way is an understandable reaction to the confines we place on ourselves and on others in our lives and to our difficulty in managing our limits and frustrations in the world. We will always have to live with it. The challenge in helping those who are suicidal is not so much to vanquish their difficulties but to help release them from the deluded idea, the fantasy, that they can be, or should be, relieved of their internal conflicts and the limitations and chaos of the world. By gaining traction on, and insight into, early experiences that have shaped and habituated their feelings we can help those tortured people amongst us respond differently to the inevitable helplessness and conflict of being in the world.

REFERENCES

Alvarez, A. (1971). *The Savage God*. London: Penguin.

Beck, A. (1991). *Beck Scale for Suicide Ideation (BSS)*. San Antonio, TX: Pearson Education.

Beck, A., Resnick, H., & Lettieri, D. (Eds.) (1974). *Development of Suicidal Intent Scales: The Prediction of Suicide*. Oxford: Charles Press.

Berryman, J. (1968). *His Toy, His Dream, His Rest*. New York: Farrar, Straus and Giroux.

Bion, W. R. (1978). *The Complete Works of W. R. Bion, Vol IX*. C. Mawson (Ed.). London: Karnac, 2014.

Bollas, C., & Sandelson, D. (1995). *The New Informants*. London: Karnac.

Bolton, J. M., Gunnell, D., & Turecki, G. (2015). Suicide risk assessment and intervention in people with mental illness. *British Medical Journal, 351*: h4978.

Boyle, M. (1988). *Schizophrenia: A Scientific Illusion*. London: Routledge.

Bristol Crisis Service for Women (1995). *Women and Self Injury Report*.

Campbell, D., & Hale, R. (1991). *Textbook of Psychotherapy in Psychiatric Practice*. J. Holmes (Ed.). London: Churchill Livingstone.

Camus, A. (1942). *The Myth of Sisyphus and Other Essays*. London: Vintage, 1991.

Cantopher, T. (2006). *Depressive Illness—Curse of the Strong*. London: Sheldon Press.

Cavell, S. (2003). *Discovering Knowledge in Seven Plays of Shakespeare (2nd edn.)*. Cambridge: Cambridge University Press.

Cole-King, A., Green, G., Gask, L., Hines, K., & Platt, S. (2013). Suicide mitigation: a compassionate approach to suicide prevention. *Advances in Psychiatric Treatment, 19*(4): 276–283.

Cole-King, A., Parker, V., Williams, H., & Platt, S. (2013). Suicide prevention: are we doing enough? *Advances in Psychiatric Treatment, 19*(4): 284–291.

Cook, R. (Intro. & Trans.) (2002). *Njal's Saga*. London: Penguin.

Department of Health (2012). *Preventing Suicide in England: A Cross-government Outcomes Strategy to Save Lives*. www.dh.gov.uk/publications (last accessed March 2016).

Diski, J. (2014). Review of *Thrive* by Leyard, R. and Clark, D. *The Guardian*, June 25.

Durkheim, E. (1897). *On Suicide: A Study of Sociology*. London: Penguin, 2006.

Fonagy, P. (1991). Thinking about thinking: Some clinical and theoretical considerations in the treatment of a borderline patient. *International Journal of Psychoanalysis, 72*: 639–656.

Fonagy, P., Gergely, G., Jurist, E. L., & Target, M. (2002). *Affect Regulation, Mentalization and the Development of the Self*. New York: Other Press.

Freud, S. (1909b). Analysis of a phobia in a five-year-old boy. *S. E., 10*. London: Hogarth.

Freud, S. (1917e). Mourning and melancholia. *S. E., 14*: 237–258. London: Hogarth.

Freud, S. (1920g). *Beyond the Pleasure Principle. S. E., 18*. London: Hogarth.

Freud, S. (1923b). *The Ego and the Id. S. E., 19*. London: Hogarth.

Freud, S. (1933a). *New Introductory Lectures on Psycho-Analysis. S. E., 22*: 1–182. London: Hogarth.

Freud, S., & Breuer, J. (1895d). *Studies on Hysteria. S. E., 2*. London: Hogarth.

Galavan, E. (2014). *Working with Suicidal Clients*. www.theprofessionalpractitioner.net (last accessed March 2016).

Gardner, F. (2001). *Self–Harm: A Psychotherapeutic Approach*. London: Routledge.

Healey, D. (2004). *Let Them Eat Prozac*. New York: New York University Press.

Holmes, J. (1996). *Attachment, Intimacy, Autonomy*. New York: Jason Aronson.

Holmes, J. (2015). Personal experience: suicide and psychiatric care—a lament. *BJPsych Bulletin, 39*: 45–47.

Jobes, D. (2006). *Managing Suicidal Risk: A Collaborative Approach*. New York: Guilford Press.

Joiner, T. E. Jr. (2005). *Why People Die by Suicide*. Cambridge, MA: Harvard University Press.

Joiner, T. E. Jr., van Orden, K. A., Witte, T. K., Selby, E. A., Ribeiro, J. D., Lewis, R., & Rudd, M. D. (2009). Main predictions of the interpersonal-psychological theory of suicidal behaviour: Empirical tests in two samples of young adults. *Journal of Abnormal Psychology, 118*(3): 634–646.

Klein, M. (1963). *Envy and Gratitude and Other Works (1946–1963)*. London: Vintage, 1997.

Leader, D. (2009). *The New Black: Mourning, Melancholia and Depression*. London: Penguin.

Leader, D. (2011). *What is Madness?* London: Penguin.

Leyard, R. (2003). *Happiness: Has Social Science a Clue?* Lionel Robbins Memorial Lecture: London School of Economics.

Leyard, R., & Clark, D. (2014). *Thrive: The Power of Psychological Therapy*. London: Penguin.

Linehan, M., Goodstein, J., Nielsen, S., & Chiles, J. (1983). Reasons for staying alive when you are thinking of killing yourself: The Reasons for Living Inventory. *Journal of Consulting and Clinical Psychology, 51*: 276–286.

Malcolm, J. (1995). *The Silent Woman: Sylvia Plath and Ted Hughes*. London: Vintage.

McManus, S., Meltzer, H., Brugha, T. S., Bebbington, P. E., & Jenkins, R. (2007). *Adult Psychiatric Morbidity: Results of a Household Survey*. London: The NHS Information Centre for Health and Social Care.

Miller, I., Norman, W., Bishop, S., & Dow, M. (1986). The Modified Scale for Suicidal Ideation: reliability and validity. *Journal of Consulting and Clinical Psychology, 54*(5): 724–725.

O'Connor, R. C. (2011). The integrated motivational-volitional model of suicidal behaviour. *Crisis: Journal of Crisis Intervention and Suicide Prevention, 32*(6): 295–298.

O'Connor, R. C., Smyth, R., Ferguson, E., Ryan, C., & Williams, J. M. G. (2013). Psychological processes and repeat suicidal behavior: A four-year prospective study. *Journal of Consulting and Clinical Psychology, 81*(6): 1137–1143.

Pasternak, B. (1959). *An Essay in Autobiography*. London: Collins and Harvill Press.

Pavese, C. (1950). *The Burning Brand Diaries 1935–1950*. New York: Walker, 1961.

Phillips, A. (1993). *On Tickling, Kissing and Being Bored*. London: Faber and Faber.

Phillips, A. (2012). *Missing Out: In Praise of the Unlived Life*. London: Hamish Hamilton.

Plato. *Phaedo*. D. Gallop (Trans.). Oxford: Oxford University Press, 2009.

Reeves, A. (2010). *Counselling Suicidal Clients*. London: Sage.

Rhodes, J. (2104). *Instrumental—A Memoir of Madness, Medication and Music.* Edinburgh: Canongate.

Roberts, S. E., Jaremin, B., & Lloyd, K. (2013). High-risk occupations for suicide. *Psychological Medicine, 43*(6): 1231–1240.

Rollins, H. E. (Ed.) (1958). *The Letters of John Keats.* Cambridge: Cambridge University Press.

Samaritans, The (2015). *Working Together to Reduce Suicide.* www.samaritans. org (last accessed March 2016).

Schopenhauer, A. (1891). *Studies in Pessimism.* New York: Cosimo Classics, 2007.

Shneidman, E. (1996). *The Suicidal Mind.* Oxford: Oxford University Press.

Stack, S., & Kposowa, A. J. (2011). Religion and suicide acceptability: A cross-national analysis. *Journal for the Scientific Study of Religion, 50*(2): 289–306.

Stengel, E. (1965). *Suicide and Attempted Suicide.* London: Penguin.

Timimi, S. (2014). No more psychiatric labels. *International Journal of Clinical and Health Psychology, 14*(3): 208–213.

Toews, M. (2014). *All My Puny Sorrows.* London: Faber and Faber.

Turp, M. (2003). *Hidden Self-Harm: Narratives from Psychotherapy.* London: Jessica Kingsley.

Van Orden, K. A., Witte, T. K., Gordon, K. H., Bender, T. W., & Joiner, T. E. Jr. (2008). Suicidal desire and the capability for suicide: Tests of the interpersonal-psychological theory of suicidal behavior among adults. *Journal of Consulting and Clinical Psychology, 76*(1): 72–83.

Wallace, D. F. (2014). *The David Foster Wallace Reader.* London: Hamish Hamilton.

Wertheimier, A. (1991). *A Special Scar.* London: Routledge.

Winnicott, D. W. (1947). Hate in the countertransference. In: *Collected Papers: Through Paediatrics to Psychoanalysis.* London: Hogarth, 1987.

Winnicott, D. W. (1956). The antisocial tendency. In: *Collected Papers: Through Paediatrics to Psychoanalysis* (pp. 306–315). London: Hogarth, 1987.

Winnicott, D. W. (1966). Psycho-somatic illness in its positive and negative aspects. In: C. Winnicott, R. Shepherd, & M. Davis (Eds.), *Psychoanalytic Explorations* (pp. 103–115). London: Karnac, 1989.

Winnicott, D. W. (1990). *Home Is Where We Start From: Essays by a Psychoanalyst.* New York: W. W. Norton.

World Health Organization (2014). *Preventing Suicide: A Global Imperative.*

INDEX

131